Any Damn Fool Can Be A Farmer

Growing Up on a Wisconsin Farm

by Bob Knopes

BADGER BOOKS, LLC
MIDDLETON, WISCONSIN

Published by Badger Books, LLC
Middleton, Wisconsin
www.badgerbooks.com
1-800-928-2372

Bob Knopes
9607 Laurel Oak Pl.
Fairfax Station , VA 22039

ISBN: 978-1-932542-35-6
Previous ISBN: 978-0-976814-60-3

Printed in the United States of America

*For my sons Christopher, Peter and Andrew
and my grandsons Archer, Elliott and Henry*

Acknowledgments

I dedicate this memoir to my parents, who encouraged and supported me in everything I did, and to my sister, Shirlee, who shared it all. When I mentioned I was thinking of writing a book about the family and the farm, Mom and Dad invited three farmer friends in to sit around the kitchen table and reminisce into a tape recorder. Tapes they made of those sessions provided me a short course in the evolution of farming in the early 20th century. On aimless rides we took around Rock County, Dad's comments on the farms and farmers we passed gave me a greater understanding of what it took to run a successful farm. And Mom was always ready to answer my questions about her life and family.

My thanks to Mary O'Leary and Dorothy Dockhorn, Mom's sisters, for sharing recollections of their parents and life in a big family on a small farm when times were tough.

Sincere thanks to my son Andrew, who edited the manuscript several times, improving it with each rewrite, and to my wife, Karen, who proofread every sentence, paragraph and chapter, correcting grammatical errors, misspellings, typos and fractured syntax.

Introduction

"Any damn fool can be a farmer," Dad often said. But we knew plenty of damn fools who tried farming and went broke because they couldn't budget time, money or resources, and didn't have the stamina or desire to work 14-hour days most of the year. Farm work was relentless, physical and difficult, but for successful farmers like Dad, farming was a calling, not just a way to earn a living.

Few things are more satisfying than seeing smooth black fields turn green as rows of new plants sprout in the spring, or seeing your barn filled with hay, your silo with corn, and your granary with golden oats at the end of the season. During the Great Depression, when money was scarce and jobs difficult to find, there was no better place to be than on a fertile farm. While people in the cities lost jobs and struggled to put food on the table, we always had work and an abundance of meat, vegetables and fruit, fresh in summer and canned in winter.

My parents were married in the fall of 1930, a year after the stock market crashed. I was born in 1932 and my sister Shirlee three years later. We grew up on a farm outside Janesville, Wisconsin, during the Depression. With the exception of Dad's Uncle Dominic, who had put his meager tailor's income into Wisconsin Power and Light stock and was wiped out and demoralized by the stock market crash of 1929, our family had no interest in stocks or bonds. The markets that concerned us were milk, hogs, and cattle.

Dad took over his parents' farm when he married, and his parents moved to town. Dad didn't have the funds to buy the farm outright, and arranged with his parents to do the work and share income and expenses 50/50 with them. Dad was a meticulous bookkeeper, filing every receipt in a kitchen drawer and writing figures with a dull pencil in a lined notebook, but he kept the overall operation in his head. The monthly milk check, which didn't approach $1,000 until 1946, was the foundation of our finances. After expenses were paid each month, the few dollars that were left over were put aside to buy a new piece of machinery or a young heifer to improve the dairy herd. If Mom wanted something for the house, she put away a few dollars each time she sold eggs or chickens. It took her more than ten years to gather funds to remodel the kitchen.

When I was born in 1932, farming was in transition from the horse power and manual labor of the 19th century to a new era of electricity and machinery. This advent of technology made farming more efficient. Milking ten cows by hand had taken an hour of strenuous squeezing but a milking machine did twice as many cows in the same amount of time, enabling farmers to build larger herds and a bigger milk check. Our tractor was slow but pulled heavier loads than any team of horses and it ran all day without rest. When Dad and two neighbors pooled resources to buy a combine and a hay baler, we could harvest oats and put hay in the barn in half the time all by ourselves; crews of 8 to 10 men that had been required to run the old machines were no longer needed. A modification as simple as replacing steel wheels with rubber tires made a wagon easier to load and to pull. Change was happening: not fast, but steadily.

We did not know, of course, as we bought the machinery that made our lives easier, that our way of life was already an anachronism. We, and our neighbors, were the last generation of the family farmers. By mid-20th century one man and his family could no longer make a living from 160-acres and a small herd of dairy cattle. The equipment that relieved farmers of the more onerous manual labor kept growing in size and efficiency until it was beyond the scale and budget of a family farm. Young men who wanted to farm began to buy up or rent land from older farmers who were retiring. Small farms like ours were melded with neighboring land to create fields of 500 or 1000 acres. Fences that had marked fields and farms disappeared. When Dad retired in 1968, combines and corn pickers were self-propelled monster machines that could harvest 100 acres in a day and dairy herds had grown to 400 or 500 head. Family farms, no longer economical or practical, began to disappear. Empty barns and decaying buildings now stand on every country road, mute reminders of the family farms that a half-century ago were the fabric of Wisconsin life.

This is the story of one family on a farm during that time of change.

Chapter 1

A Working Farm

*F*arm life was a quiet life. Except for the steady drone of tractors during the day and the sounds of animals and insects at night, there was silence. Few cars came down our dirt road — four or five on the busiest day, and that included the mailman in the morning and the guy who threw the tightly wrapped *Janesville Daily Gazette* into our driveway in the afternoon. In summer, our neighbors the Liptows, whose rented farm was too small to devote any land to pasture, let their cattle graze along the road without fear of cars or trucks coming by. There was so little traffic that I yelled, "Here comes a car!" any time I saw a rooster-plume of dust moving along our road. I would stop what I was doing to follow its progress, hoping it would turn into our driveway.

Our section of road (now Highway 14, then called Humes Road) was two miles long, from Highway 26 on the west to Townline Road on the east. There were three farms on the south side and six on the north, including ours. Our property was about an eighth of a mile wide and a mile long, bounded on the north by Rotamer Road. The gravel road was dusty in summer, frozen solid in winter and tough driving all year round. Riding a steel-wheeled wagon over that washboard road made your joints hurt and shook the hat right off your head. A neighbor, Mark Campbell, who had bad knees, showed me how to stand with legs bent to absorb some of the shock. Two or three times a year a county road grader came by, its big blade smoothing out the washboard, but the next time it rained the road returned to its corrugated, car-rattling, passenger-jarring mode.

When I was growing up, our barn was the newest and best equipped on the road. This was because, in the fall of 1932, when I was just six months old, sparks from a steam engine started a fire that destroyed all our buildings, sparing only the house, granary and garage. Compared to our neighbors' aging, weathered farm buildings, the bright red and white trim of ours sparkled in the sun and captured the eye of everyone who drove down our road.

Barn fires were not uncommon. Lightning strikes, kerosene lanterns and careless smoking sparked many. The steam engines that provided power for large farm equipment — threshing machines, silo fillers and corn shredders — ignited their share, too. Steam engines were a common sight in summer and fall, spouting soot and sparks from their big smokestacks as they crept along the gravel road on steel wheels six-feet tall. The engineer tooted the steam whistle a mile down the road so the farmer would have his machinery ready to go when the engine pulled into the driveway. The same whistle let the farmer's wife know she would have a crew of workers to feed for a couple of days.

The steam engine was placed thirty to forty feet from the thresher or silo filler and its flywheel was connected to the pulley of the other machine by a long canvas belt. The engineer kept the firebox stoked with wood and a water boy made sure the reservoir always had plenty of water. Soot from the smokestack mingled with dust from the fields and chaff from the thresher, while the noise from the spinning belt, working machinery and hissing steam kept conversation to an occasional shout.

In the fall of 1932, one of these smoke-belching monsters set up next to our barn, its big fly wheel powering the silo filler that cut bundles of corn into one-inch pieces of silage and blew them 40 feet up a pipe into the concrete silo.

Intent on getting loads of corn into the silo as quickly as possible, no one paid attention to drifting sparks from the boiler stack. It was Mom, coming out of the chicken house with a basket of eggs, who saw the sparks land on the dry shingles of the barn and begin to smolder. In a few moments the shingles were ablaze and embers began dropping through the roof, into the hayloft, igniting the hay. Dry timbers, a mow full of hay and years of accumulated dust provided ready fuel. The barn disappeared in smoke and flame.

The machine shed was next to go. Set afire by flying embers, it burned briskly then collapsed on machinery stored for the winter. Then the tobacco shed blazed and the just-harvested crop was turned into a smoldering green pile. The straw pile behind the barn blazed, adding a plume of white smoke to the ugly gray and black from the barn and tobacco shed. Nothing could be done about the buildings already engulfed in flame, but men got ladders and buckets and began to wet down the roof of the house while others carried furniture out to the lawn. When it appeared nothing could be saved, the wind shifted, carrying the flying sparks away from the house and granary. By the time fire trucks arrived from Janesville, the damage had been done. There was little for them to do but wet down the ashes.

In less than an hour, we had lost our livelihood. Half our machinery sat in the ashes, blackened and twisted pieces of useless metal. The year's harvest of hay, tobacco, and silage corn was gone. Only the animals, who had been in the pasture during the blaze, and the oats in the granary, were saved. Despite the tremendous shock, there was little question about what to do. The land was still fertile, the buildings were insured, and the dairy herd had survived. We would start over. Before the day was out, a generous neighbor, who no longer kept a herd of cows, loaned us his barn and through the winter Dad commuted four miles round trip twice a day to feed and milk the cows.

Debris was hauled to the dump, lumber ordered for new buildings and a crew of carpenters hired. The country was in an economic depression, so labor was plentiful and cheap. Dad said, "I paid skilled carpenters 35 cents an hour and laborers 10 cents less, and they were glad to get the work." By the spring of 1933, new crops were planted and the new barn — solid and imposing, 90 feet long and 40 feet wide, running due east and west — had risen from the ashes.

The barn took on color as it neared completion. The concrete foundation walls were whitewashed, the wood sides painted bright red and the windows trimmed bright white. Inside were four pens on the east end — three for calves and one with extra strong bars for the bull — and on the west were four wooden horse stalls and a storage room for ground feed. On each side of the barn was a row of 12 steel stanchions for the cows, with a concrete manger in front and a gutter in back. A driveway ran through the middle of the barn, wide enough to accommodate a team of horses and a manure spreader.

The Knopes farm - 1955

After the fire

The floor of the haymow above rested on two beams of six 2 x 8 planks bolted together that ran the length of the barn. These beams were supported by steel posts set every 10 feet in the concrete floor. In the spring the haymow was a vast empty space that I used as my playground, climbing the rafters and swinging on the hay rope. In the fall, the supporting beams groaned and sagged under tons of fresh hay and straw we had packed right to the roof over the summer.

Before we filled the barn with hay the first time, Dad installed a 500-gallon steel tank in the haymow to supply water to the automatic drinking cups located next to each cow's stanchion. When a cow pushed down on the lever in the bottom of the cup with her nose, a valve opened and water flowed down from the tank. Our cows had running water long before we had that luxury in the house.

The tank was also a convenience for our hired man, who regularly filled his cup from the faucet in the barn. He often remarked that this was the sweetest water he had ever tasted. One day, when the flow slowed to a trickle, he and Dad uncovered the tank to see why and found a drowned rat plugging the pipe. The hired man's cup disappeared from its hook next to the faucet and from then on he never minded having to go to the well to get a drink of water.

After the fire, the farm was a mixture of old and new. We had a new barn but an old house. The garage had escaped without damage, while the granary, the building nearest the barn, was scorched but saved. As for the rest of the buildings — the chicken house, corn crib, pig pen and machine shed — they all had to be replaced. Dad decided not to rebuild the tobacco shed because several neighbors had unused sheds and were willing to share the space.

A steam engine like the one that set our barn on fire

As on most Wisconsin farms, the buildings were built around a gravel yard that was the center of activity, both a transit point and a parking area. When we hosted a holiday dinner our yard was filled with cars. On work days we parked wagons there between jobs and tanked up the tractor at the gas pump next to the milk house. We pulled loads of hay and grain through the yard on the way to the barn and the granary, and machinery passed through on the way to the field beyond the barn. The yard was bounded by the garage and granary on the west, the house to the south, the barn to the north, and the milk house to the east. The new machine shed, which Dad built himself, was beyond the barnyard to the east. Dad made the shed big enough to hold all our machinery, but fitting in the plows, the combine, the hay loader, the wagons, and the tractor was like assembling a large jigsaw puzzle. It took a lot of planning and maneuvering.

A board fence ran from the milk house to the barn to hide the mud and weeds of the barnyard where the cows gathered before milking. Next to the milk house was the windmill that supplied water for all farm activities. Every morning and evening after milking, Dad engaged the gears that connected the wind vanes at the top of the windmill to the pump below, bringing cool water up from the well to flow around the cans of fresh milk he had lowered into the tank in the milk house. When the milk house tank was full, the water ran out an overflow pipe into the stock tank outside. Turning a valve at the pump sent water through a pipe across the yard into the tank in the haymow of the barn.

The driveway from the road opened onto the graveled yard. People who knew us drove in and parked by the door to the entryway, where we kept our coats and galoshes in winter and where Dad hung his work clothes every day. They opened the kitchen door and walked in, yelling, "Anybody home?" Strangers knocked on the entryway door, not knowing a major pounding was required to be heard in the kitchen. Only salesmen new to the route went to the side door to the kitchen, a door that we never used and opened only in summer for ventilation. Dad built a picket fence and planted flowers and grass by that door to make the area more attractive and to direct visitors to the entry way.

The gravel yard was also my playground. It was there I learned to ride my bike and where I took my first rides on my pony. I played ball games by myself, throwing a ball up on the slanted barn roof and trying to catch it on the fly when it came down. In winter, when the north wind blew the snow over the wood fence, drifts several feet deep filled the yard. Digging tunnels and sliding on the snow was great fun for us kids, but for Dad it was just extra work having to dig pathways to the garage, chicken house and barn.

Between the house and the road was a lawn of thick grass, which we called the front yard. When Shirl and I were small it was fenced, making an enclosed space where Mom could keep an eye on us as she sat on the screened porch. On hot summer days we cooled off in a metal wash tub she filled with water. Dad hung a swing from one of the tall elm trees by the road and we played croquet and catch on the lawn when friends came to visit.

There was a light on the corner of the barn that illuminated the yard as we finished up milking and other chores in winter. We left it on until we went to bed to let those who drove by know that we were home and they were welcome to drop in if they had the time.

Our neighbors across the road did not have electric lights. Compared to other farms on our road they were still living in the 19th century, relying on a team of horses to do all the field work on the eighty acres they rented, and milking their small dairy herd by hand. In the evening when I looked across the road, I saw the ghostly movement of lanterns as the men moved across the yard to the barn to begin milking. At dusk, the feeble light of kerosene lamps began to flicker through the windows of their house. Later in the evening the light faded from the downstairs windows and reappeared in upstairs rooms as the family prepared for bed. The floating lights were an eerie sight and I thought how difficult it must be to read and do homework by the light of a lamp.

In the early 1950's our road was paved and became U.S. Highway 14. Highway 14 had always been the major north-south artery from Chicago to Madison, passing through downtown Janesville. As a growing number of large trucks and weekend travel brought congestion, tie-ups, and accidents, the road was rerouted north of the city, and Humes Road became a major thoroughfare. It took some time, but we got used to the speeding cars and the giant trucks that rattled our windows as they worked their gears up to cruising speed after the stop light a mile west at Highway 26. But, living on a paved highway relieved us of dust from passing traffic in summer and guaranteed that snowplows opened our road first after a blizzard.

Dad on his way to the barn - 1971

One day we saw cars on the highway swerving left and right, trying to avoid something moving in the road. It was a black cocker spaniel with a distinctive white patch over one eye, sauntering down the middle of the road, clearly unconcerned by the rushing traffic around him. Without encouragement from us, the little dog turned into our drive-way and trotted up to the house as though he were coming home. Dad fed him and named him George. Our farm became his home and he never left again, except in the passenger seat of Dad's pickup truck on his many trips to town. We had always had a dog, usually a large one that herded the cows and acted as watchdog. George, if coaxed, would bark at the cows to get them moving, but he was generally indifferent to what was happening around him. What he did have was a sense that alerted him whenever Dad planned to go somewhere in the truck. Even before Dad moved toward the garage, George would be sitting by the truck, ready to leap up on the seat as soon as Dad opened the door. Then off they would go, like an old couple on a Sunday drive — Dad with an unlit cigar in his teeth and George sitting, head erect, eyes on the road, on the passenger side. Wherever they ended up — at the feed mill, at a bar, or at a hardware store — George would wait patiently in the truck until Dad returned.

Chapter 2

Cows and Crops

Spring was the busiest, and in many ways the happiest, season of the farm year. We took off our winter coats and felt the rising warmth of the sun. Green sprouts peeked through the brown residue of last year's grass. Apple and cherry trees bloomed with pink and white blossoms, the lilac bushes in the front yard flaunted a profusion of purple, and the white flowers of bridal wreath bushes blossomed next to the front porch. Our house was filled with the fragrance of spring.

Spring affected the animals, too. The cattle, confined in the barn through the winter, were delighted when turned loose to soak up sunshine and graze on the tender new grass in the pasture. One March, after the ice had melted in the watering tank by the milk house, Dad suggested I take the horses outside to drink, rather than bringing buckets of water to them in their stalls as I had done during the winter. I untied Bob, a dappled gray gelding, and led him out of the barn and across the graveled yard to the tank. After taking a long drink, Bob suddenly tossed his head and kicked his hind legs high in the air. When his hind legs came down he rose up on his front legs, lifting me off the ground. I tried to hold tight to the halter rope, but, when my feet left the ground for the second time, I let go and scurried away. Bob bucked and pranced his way around the yard for only a minute or two, then stopped, gathered himself, and walked back to his stall to calmly begin munching a mouthful of hay. When harnessed to a wagon, Bob was a strong and stolid worker, never balking or bolting. But for a few minutes on that spring day he showed an exuberance that was both delightful and scary to an eight-year-old (who was supposed to be in charge).

Lil, the other half of our team of horses, never showed an independent spirit. She was such a gentle and placid mare that, when I was very young, Dad sometimes lifted me up on her back and led her around the yard. When I was six, he put a bridle on her and let me ride alone. There was no saddle made that would span her broad expanse, so I rode bareback, legs splayed out almost horizontally. My rides around the yard became so routine that one day Mom put me up on Lil and sent me down the road to borrow some brushes from a neighbor. On the way back Lil was spooked by a passing car and began to run for home. I pulled on the reins and frantically yelled "Whoa!" but Lil paid no attention. When we reached our driveway Lil made a sharp right turn, heading for the barn, and I flew forward, into a ditch. I woke up on the living room couch with scratches and bruises, Mom frantically dabbing at my forehead with a damp cloth.

My wild ride awakened me to the fact that farm activities could turn bad quickly. Indeed, I was to witness this many times during my years on the farm. Our neighbor's twelve-year-old son was killed when he fell from the hay loft onto a pitchfork. At 4-H camp I roomed with a young man who had run across the hay field into the path of the horse-drawn mower his father was driving. The horses bolted and the sickle cut off his arm and almost severed his leg, as well. An elderly friend of Dad's was killed when his trouser leg caught in the rapidly spinning power takeoff as he stepped off the tractor. Danger lay in wait for farmers of any age, and there were always lessons to be learned — often the hard way.

Not long after that wild ride Dad bought me a pony and saddle. At 6, my legs were still too short to reach the wooden stirrups, so Dad stuffed my feet into the straps above them and I was soon riding to the woods to bring the cows home for milking. Every afternoon as I saddled up, I hoped to find the cows still grazing among the trees in the woods so I could round them up, just like a real cowboy, but I always found them resting contentedly by the muddy pond, chewing their cuds. That didn't stop me from doing my cowboy imitation, circling them, shouting and waving my arms until they were on their feet and headed down the fenced lane to the barn. The cows spent the night in the pasture behind the barn and didn't need to be herded in the morning. Sometimes, when I was still in bed, I heard Dad call into the darkness, "C'a boss, c'a boss" to rouse them and let them know there was fresh feed waiting for them in the mangers. That's all that was needed to get them moving to the barn in the morning.

My earliest jobs had to do with the barn and the cows. To keep flies from congregating in the barn in summer, every morning I swept the floor and covered it with lime to soak up any moisture. In the evening, when the cows were locked in their stanchions and ready for milking, I closed the barn doors and sprayed insecticide in the air and on the back and belly of each cow to kill the flies they had carried in from the field. Killing the flies lessened the need for the cows to flick their tails to clear the pesky insects from their backs. And the more flies I could kill, the easier it was to attach the milking machine without getting whacked in the face by a rapidly moving — and usually very dirty — cow tail.

Our house

Dad showed me how to approach a cow. "Move in slowly from the side," he said, "so you're out of range of the hooves. Always make some sound, like 'Soo, boss,' to let her know you're there." He continued, "Keep to the side and touch her lightly on the rump, then push hard against her hip to keep her off balance. She can't kick when she's off balance. Then you can reach down and attach the suction cups to her teats." That's the way I did it and I was never kicked by a cow. I forgot the rule once and was kicked soundly by a horse when I came up behind it too fast and too quietly. That helped me remember Dad's rule.

Cows loved the fresh grass in our woods and pastures but their real treat was the ground feed (a mixture of ground corn and oats, fortified with minerals and vitamins) they got before milking. Every afternoon, winter and summer, I filled a wheelbarrow with ground feed and put a scoop in the concrete manger in front of each cow. In winter, when there was no grass and the cows were inside all day, I added a forkful of silage for each cow's afternoon meal. Then I went to the milk house, assembled the two milking machines, and carried them and four 12-gallon milk cans to the barn so everything was ready for Dad to begin milking.

Through the day and much of the night the cows ate, drank and chewed their cud, calmly and serenely making milk. Their four stomachs and intestinal tract were in constant action as they converted food to milk. But not all they ate became milk; much passed through their systems and was deposited in the gutters behind them.

The driveway through the middle of the barn made these gutters easy to clean. Every morning in winter our team of horses pulled the manure spreader through the barn and we used a five-tined fork, the width of the gutter, to load the manure into the spreader. Efficient loading took strength and concentration! You load the fork, swing it forward with arms and shoulders, and turn it as it cleared the side of the manure spreader so the entire load fell inside. I shoveled from the right, Dad from the left. The horses were attentive and when they heard a quiet "giddyup" they moved forward a few steps so we didn't have to pause in our work. At the end of the gutter we quickly scooped up the liquid residue with a shovel, threw it into the spreader and sent the horses out the door before it began to leak out of the wooden bottom of the spreader.

The Knopes farm

I usually drove the loaded manure spreader out to the field. In the field I engaged a set of gears that started a conveyor in the bottom of the spreader. The conveyor carried the manure slowly back to two sets of rotating beaters which spread the load smoothly and evenly over the ground. One day, with a strong wind at my back, I engaged the gear as usual, but quickly sensed that something was wrong. I felt a sensation on my back, as though someone was throwing clods of dirt at me. I stopped the horses and looked around, but there was no one near. Was I imagining things? I took off my cap and found it was covered with manure. The mystery was suddenly solved. The wind was so strong that it was carrying the airborne particles of manure forward. I learned that day to always check the direction of the wind before putting the spreader in gear — a lesson that was useful during my later career in government.

After major snowstorms, the loaded manure spreader was too heavy for the horses to pull through the drifts. So we hitched the team to a sledge, a wagon box mounted on steel-covered wooden runners, which we usually used to bring logs down from the woods. The sledge moved easily over the snow, but even our strong team could not pull it over the concrete driveway of the barn. Dad solved the problem by placing sections of one-inch pipe under the runners to act as small wheels. As the sledge moved forward the pipes rolled under the runners, front to rear. When a pipe rolled out the back, I picked it up and placed it again at the front, careful to keep my fingers out of harm's way.

We didn't like to use the sledge because it had no conveyor belt or beaters. The manure had to be unloaded by hand, thrown into the air — forkful by forkful — so it was spread evenly over the ground. In small amounts, manure is fertilizer and good for crops. If dumped in thick clumps it cuts off air and sun, preventing plants from taking hold in the spring.

When blizzards piled snowdrifts so deep the team couldn't get beyond the barnyard, we loaded the sledge, took it as far from the barn as the horses could manage, and threw the manure into a pile, where it remained, frozen solid over the winter. With the spring thaw, before it began to smell and collect flies, we loaded the pile into the spreader and spread it over the fields.

Taking out the manure was a smelly, tedious, seven-day-a-week winter job. (In summer the cows were in the barn only twice a day for milking, so the gutters needed cleaning only once a week.) In 1951, after I had joined the navy, Dad installed a barn cleaner — a set of paddles powered by a big electric motor that moved the manure through the gutters, up a chute and into the spreader. You just parked the spreader under the chute, turned on the motor and let the paddles do the work. Even liquids were carried up and out of the barn. After he got the barn cleaner, Dad gladly retired the five-tine manure fork.

Cash crops, such as tobacco, peas and sugar beets, brought in supplemental income each year, but milk provided us with our regular income. Before electricity and mechanical milkers, cows were milked by hand. A man could milk five or six cows an hour, so herds were small and most of the milk was used on the farm for drinking and making butter. A milking machine enabled a farmer to milk a herd of 25 or 30 cows in an hour, providing all the milk he needed and plenty left to sell.

Our first milking machine (at least the first one I remember) milked two cows at once. A pump by the barn door created a vacuum that ran through pipes above the cows' mangers. The milking machine was connected to the vacuum pipe with a long hose; a valve on the machine alternated suction and relaxation in the four cups attached to the cow's teats, top to bottom. This action squeezed the milk from the teats, just as a human hand would do. Two good milk cows filled the 3-gallon bucket in about five minutes. We poured the milk through a strainer into the 12-gallon milk cans set up at the end of the barn. After milking, we pushed the cans of fresh milk across the yard to the milk house in a steel-wheeled cart, set the cans in the water tank and started the windmill to begin a flow of cold water to cool the milk so it wouldn't sour.

In summer we finished milking in little over an hour and turned the cows out into the pasture for the night. In winter, evening chores took longer because the cows remained in the barn and had to be fed hay and bedded down for the night. That became my job, climbing the ladder into the hay mow to throw down straw for bedding and hay to fill the mangers.

Dad did the milking early in the morning. Until I was about 14, he did it by himself, letting me sleep until after the sun was up. In winter, I got up and got ready for school. In summer, after milking was done, he rousted me out of bed by 7:00 a.m. to begin work in the field. When we agreed it was time for me to help with morning milking, Dad woke me the first day at 5:30 a.m., before he went to the barn. He returned a half-hour later to see what was keeping me and found me half dressed, a sock in my hand, asleep again on the unmade bed. He shook me awake but by the time I got to the barn he had about finished milking and it was time for me to get ready for school. He tried again the next morning, with the same result, then gave up. He wasn't angry or disgusted with my lack of response. He just decided it wasn't worth the time and effort to hold me to the plan. In the time he spent walking back and forth to the house to get me moving, he could milk four cows. I continued to sleep in and Dad did the morning milking.

I started feeding the chickens and gathering eggs when I was about six. Scooping ground feed from a 50-gallon barrel and pouring it into four-foot-long metal feeders was fairly simple, but gathering eggs was not quite as easy. The old biddy hens were protective of the eggs they laid, expecting to sit on them until they hatched. They tried to thwart anything or anyone that attempted to remove their eggs. The sharp, quick pecks they gave were more startling than painful, but I dropped plenty of eggs until I got used to the jabs. I am not sure one ever really gets used to something like that. I would be apprehensive even now if I were asked to reach toward a nest guarded by an old hen.

We did not have running water in our house until 1945, when I was 13. Until then we kept a bucket of drinking water and a dipper on a shelf behind the stove in the kitchen. As soon as I was big enough to carry a bucket, I got the job of going to the well to refill it. On breezy days I just hung the empty pail on the pump spigot, pulled down on the handle that started the windmill, and waited for the water to flow. On still days, when there was no wind, I grabbed the pump handle and worked it up and down until the pail was full. Then I lifted the bucket off the pump, held it with both hands between my legs, and duck-walked it to the kitchen door, where Mom waited to put it on the shelf. Even after I was strong enough to carry the bucket in one hand, I sometimes ended up with a shoeful of water as I struggled to maintain my balance.

I got my first important job (at least I considered it most important) when I was about 10, driving the truck while Dad loaded hay onto it. I had driven the team of horses on the hay wagon the year before, but horses have a sense of the job and need minimal guidance to follow windrows of hay around the field. When Dad decided to use the truck instead of the horse-drawn wagon for haying, I was still the designated driver. When I got behind the wheel of the truck I was aware of one major difference. The team of horses stopped when I pulled on the reins and yelled, "Whoa!" The truck would only stop if I pushed in the clutch or the brake. I couldn't reach either one. "In an emergency, just turn off the ignition," Dad told me as he pulled out the dashboard throttle, put the truck in low gear and let out the clutch. "Drive straight ahead and keep the radiator cap lined up with the windrow of hay," he said, then stepped up on the truck bed and waited for the hay to come up the slatted conveyor of the hay loader as the truck moved forward, straddling the windrow of hay.

When driving the horses I stood in the front of the wagon, holding the reins, Dad stacking the hay just behind me. I felt like a real member of the team. Sitting in the truck cab on that first day, however, I felt alone and anxious. I resolved to keep the radiator cap aligned with the row of hay as Dad told me to, but I worried about the turns at the end of the field. Windrows of hay are raked in continuous circles, the rows growing shorter and the turns sharper as we moved to the middle of the field. The turns had to be wide enough so the loader tracked over the windrow on the corners. "Go past the row a few feet and then begin your turn," Dad shouted. "Don't worry if you miss some. We'll pick it up on the final load." I eyed the distance and began pulling the big wheel around, straining, using all my strength. I turned the first corner, straightened out the wheels, and lined up again on the windrow. Success! I was driving the truck! I finished that day with no mishaps and a real sense of accomplishment.

I soon gained so much confidence that I began to think I could handle the old truck any time, any place, and Dad began to trust my truck driving skills more and more. One time, later that summer, he set the throttle, put the truck in gear, and sent me home from the field with a load of grain. "The turn around the windmill is too sharp for you to make so don't try to drive to the granary," Dad warned me as he sent me on my way. "Park the truck behind the barn." As the truck crept along in low gear, I decided it was the perfect time to show him just how good a driver I had become. I would take the truck directly to the granary. I knew it would be difficult; If I turned too soon, the truck would catch the corner of the windmill: If I turned too late, I would hit the picket fence by the house. But I knew how to drive so didn't give these problems a second thought. What I didn't know was just how heavy a load of grain was and that most of the weight is on the front wheels (making it harder to turn).

I started the turn to the granary a little late, in an effort to avoid the windmill. It was soon clear that the truck was not coming around fast enough. In fact, it wasn't coming around much at all. I was headed right for the picket fence and the house. I strained harder at the wheel, but I had no leverage — my feet didn't reach the floor. I was still pulling on the wheel when I heard the gate post crack and the low fence crunch under the front tires. Horrified, I wondered if the truck would just keep going, straight into the kitchen?

When the front tire came up against the bottom step, the motor stalled, thankfully, and the truck stopped. In the sudden silence, I sat petrified, my hands still on the steering wheel. I didn't know what to expect, but whatever it was, it would have to wait. I opened the door of the truck and ran out into the cornfield to hide, wondering why I hadn't just turned off the engine with the key when things started to go wrong.

At dinner time I went back to house, ready to accept my punishment. To my surprise, my destructive drive wasn't mentioned at dinner that night or any time after. Dad didn't punish mistakes in judgment. I think he considered them learning opportunities. When the oats crop were harvested and in the granary, Dad rebuilt the fence and I helped paint it white.

Over the years jobs kept coming. Some were fun, like trimming the cows' shanks with big electric clippers in the fall (so manure would not collect in their hair while they stood idle in their stalls over winter), and teaching calves to drink by putting three fingers in their mouths and lowering my hand into a pail of milk as they sucked. Some jobs were tough and dirty — like cleaning the accumulation of chicken droppings from under the roosts of the chicken house, with chickens underfoot raising a cloud of smelly dust. Some were just boring — like daily sweeping of the barn in summer, washing the milking machines and unloading grain.

A job that tightened me with fear was fence building. Every spring Dad observed, "Some of the line fence is down again. Bob, put a roll of barbed wire and the tools in the truck. We'll fix the broken section, then build a new fence across the pasture." I didn't mind the physical side of fence building - digging holes for the wooden posts or driving steel posts three feet into the ground - but barbed wire was mean stuff. I had seen the damage it did to animals that had run into it in a panic. I imagined what it would do to me if it snapped while I was tightening it along a fence line.

I preferred setting up an electric fence - driving steel posts into the ground, attaching a single strand of barbed wire with insulators, and hooking up a battery to send a pulse of electricity through the wire to shock any animal that brushed against it. This was a temporary and effective way to partition a pasture for cattle, but it would not keep a herd of cows out of a corn field. Only a solid woven wire fence could do that. (I told my city cousin that peeing on the electric fence was harmless and encouraged him to see for himself, but he never did.)

A line fence of woven wire, fastened every five yards to wood or steel posts, with two or three strands of barbed wire along the top to deter cattle from reaching over and gradually pushing it down, would last for years. Each strand of barbed wire was pulled taut with a wire stretcher before being attached to the post. I worked the wire stretcher, ratcheting it tighter and tighter as Dad tested the tension along the fence. When I thought the wire was plenty taut, Dad would say, "Give it a couple more turns to be sure," and I would cautiously pull again on the handle, certain that this time the wire would snap, lacerating my neck and body. Fortunately, it never happened. My only accident in fence building was catching my hand between a ten-pound post driver and a steel post, stripping the skin from my palm. The accident wouldn't have caused nearly as much damage if I had taken the time to put on leather gloves .

The job I hated most was castrating the young male pigs.

I shivered when Dad opened a pack of single blade safety razors and said, "Well, Bob, it's time to cut the pigs." My job was to catch the victim, flip him upside down and immobilize him in a triangle-shaped feeding trough while Dad removed his testicles with the razor blade. I sat on the squealing animal and faced away from the operation so I wouldn't see the cutting and the blood. It was a great relief to me when I released the last pig and he ran off into the pasture. Dad never suggested that I learn the procedure. He must have known how queasy I felt about the job.

Holding the heads of heifers still while Dad sawed off their budding horns was another task I would have liked to pass up. But, it was one of those jobs that had to be done and there was no one else around to do it. During the process I was able to convince myself that, since Dad was sawing through horn, not skin, and there was little blood, it was a painless procedure. I still hope my rationalization was correct.

Chapter 3

The House

The barn was new, but the house, built in the late 1800's, was showing its age. "Too damn bad the house didn't burn, too," opined Grandpa Fanning, who arrived after the fire was under control. That sentiment may have been too strong, but Mom often wondered what it would have been like if the house had been rebuilt, too. (Sixty-five years later, when the state of Wisconsin took the old farmhouse to widen Highway 14, she got a new house, using the money the state paid for the old house to build a bungalow on a lot she owned on Rotamer Road.) The fire had spared our 50-year-old, two-story frame house, which was well-constructed but poorly insulated. In the two-story part of the house was a dining room, living room or parlor, and a downstairs bedroom. Upstairs were four unheated bedrooms. A small entryway and large kitchen comprised the single-story section of the house, which must have been added as an afterthought. Under the main part of the house was a dirt-floor basement. Over the winter the front part of the room held a bin of potatoes, barrels of apples and shelves laden with Mason jars filled with fruits and vegetables Mom had canned. In the back was a cast-iron, wood-burning furnace, which was later converted to coal, and later still to oil. It was a big old house, short on conveniences and comforts — like running water, plumbing, efficient heating and insulation — but it provided shelter and security for us.

In those days, furnaces did not have fans to force warm air through the pipes. The heat rose by convection into the living and dining rooms directly above. The kitchen was warmed by the big cook stove. When the furnace was blazing, air hot enough to bake apples came up through the register. When the fire waned, the rooms cooled quickly and Dad would say, "Bob, you better go down and throw a couple of chunks in the furnace." I didn't mind that job. I liked opening the iron door, stirring the embers with a long poker and filling the fire pot with chunks of wood that barely fit through the 2-by-2-foot opening. I sometimes buried the poker in the coals until the tip glowed bright red, then used it to burn patterns in a piece wood. Other times I stood by the open door, watching the flames curl around the chunks of wood, thinking this must be like the fires of hell the nuns told us we would suffer if we didn't learn our catechism lessons.

Before going to bed, Dad added wood and banked the coals to keep the fire burning overnight. Even so, there was little heat left in the old house when he got up at 5 a.m. Only a few embers remained in the ashes of the furnace and the wood stove in the kitchen had gone out completely. Dad got them both burning strong before he went out to feed and milk the cows. By the time Shirl and I raced down the steps from our unheated upstairs bedrooms, the first-floor was warm again.

Both the furnace and the cook stove were stoked with firewood Dad cut in our woods. Each winter, he and a hired man hitched the horses to the sledge, took a tin bucket of coffee and some sandwiches, and drove through the snow across the fields to the woods. Dad picked out a couple of trees to cut and he and the hired man set to work. They used double-bitted axes to fell the trees and trim off the branches, then cut the trunks into twelve-foot lengths with a crosscut saw. The saw, five-feet long with deep teeth and a handle on each end, cut in both directions as the two men pulled it back and forth through the tree trunk.

I sometimes went along on these expeditions, but it was cold for a non-worker. I was too small to wield an ax or pull the crosscut saw so I didn't get the exercise needed to raise my body heat. The best I could do was run around gathering chips and twigs so Dad could build a fire to warm our hands and heat the coffee and cocoa we drank with our sandwiches at lunch time. As I watched Dad work I looked forward to the day I would be big enough to grasp one end of the saw and swing my shoulders, pulling and pushing the serrated teeth through the log, watching a mound of sawdust build underneath. But, by the time I could swing an ax or wield a saw, we were burning coal in our furnace and Mom was cooking with a propane stove.

We sat on the load of logs as the horses pulled us home across the snow. Dad piled the logs next to the house and, during the winter, cut them into two-foot chunks, pushed them through the cellar window, and stacked them next to the furnace. He used an ax to split some of the chunks into sticks and stacked these next to the outhouse. When the wood box in the entryway was empty, it was my job to replenish it. It took two or three trips to fill an empty wood box. When the woodpile was bound together with snow and ice after a blizzard, it took a lot of kicking and pounding to break loose enough pieces from the frozen heap to keep up with Mom's need for wood. When I was struggling with those armloads of wood I thought about Dad's story of the bachelor farmer who inserted one end of a 10-foot log in the firebox of the cook stove and supported the other end on the back of a chair. As the log burned, he pushed it forward into the stove, so he didn't have to carry frozen sticks to keep warm. I thought it was an innovative idea but I knew it wasn't worth suggesting it for our kitchen.

My first pony

The furnace did a passable job of keeping the downstairs warm, but there were no hot air pipes to carry warmth to the upstairs bedrooms. When it was ten degrees below zero outside, the temperature in my bedroom was below freezing. Dad told me that when he was young he warmed his sheets with a pan filled with hot coals before getting into bed. For some reason that humanitarian practice had been abandoned and I always had to climb into a cold bed. My technique was to toast myself over the hot air register in the dining room, then race up the stairs and crawl under the covers while my flannel pajamas were still warm. Snuggled under layers of woolen blankets and down comforters, I could ignore the cold until morning. During blizzards, when the wind howled around the corners of the house and hard snow crackled against the window panes, I sometimes lay awake, fearing that the window would break, the fury of the storm would race into my room, and in the morning Mom would find her son frozen solid and covered with snow. But in that solid house, my fear was unfounded.

When I woke on winter mornings I lay in bed, watching my breath as I exhaled, admiring the intricate tracings of frost on the still-intact windows. I reached a hand from under the covers to warm my cold nose, steeling myself to throw back the covers and expose myself to the icy air. I stayed in bed as long as possible, ignoring Mom's warning shouts that I would be late for school. Just before she made good on her threat to come up and drag me out, I grabbed my clothes and dashed down the stairs to the kitchen to dress in front of the open oven door.

Dad had finished milking and had eaten by the time Shirl and I were ready for breakfast. The aroma of bacon and eggs — Dad's usual breakfast — was still in the air as we sat down for our breakfast of orange and banana slices, toast and cereal. On winter mornings I dipped butter-coated saltine crackers in a cup of warm milk that was laced with enough coffee to change the color and so much sugar it didn't all dissolve. Though we operated a dairy farm, we drank little milk. Cream was what we liked. Each morning Mom went to the milk house and skimmed several cups of the heavy cream from the cans of milk before the milkman came to take them away. We put cream on our cereal and poured it over strawberries, raspberries and peaches. Dad used it in his coffee, Mom cooked with it and whipped it into a solid, puffy mass that she mounded up on cakes and pies.

Through the summer, as different fruits and vegetables came into season, Mom stoked up the cook stove and set cauldrons of water boiling to clean and sterilize Mason jars and lids and to steam, stew, blanch, scald or parboil the corn, peas, beans, tomatoes, peaches, pears, raspberries, strawberries, apples, cherries and cucumbers that would fill those Mason jars and feed us through the winter.

While the water was heating we shelled the peas, peeled the tomatoes, cored the apples, husked the corn, topped the strawberries, scrubbed the cucumbers or pitted the cherries to be canned that day. Tomatoes were scalded and peeled, then canned whole or squeezed through a colander for tomato juice. Raspberries and strawberries Mom turned into jams and jellies. Cucumbers were treated according to their size. Large ones were soaked in brine and canned with sprigs of dill; mediums were sliced thin for bread-and-butter pickles; and the smallest left whole, soaked in sugar and spices to make sweet pickles.

Except for a bushel of peaches we bought from a grocer in town, everything Mom canned came from our fields. Grape vines grew on the fence behind the garage, cherry and apple trees bloomed on either side of the house and Dad tilled and tended a garden that provided tomatoes, beans, sweet corn and beets. Mom picked and cooked the wild asparagus and rhubarb that grew up along the fence rows every year, and, in July, raspberries and gooseberries on wild bushes in the woods and along the fence lines ripened in profusion. As I brought the cows home in the evening, I stopped to eat them right off the bushes that grew along the lane.

To pick the raspberries that grew wild in our woods, we dressed in wide-brimmed hats, long sleeves, and gloves and scarves to protect as much skin as possible from the fierce mosquitoes that filled the air. We tied our pant legs at the bottom with binder twine to keep biting insects from attacking. Swathed in this heavy clothing, with sweat running down our backs and mosquitoes buzzing around our heads, we made our way from bush to bush, filling buckets that were tied to our belts (so both hands would be free for picking). The berry season was short and we had only a few days to pick as many as possible. Those we weren't able to pick were eaten by birds or quickly dried up into tasteless, seedy nuggets. During the berry season we ate berries morning, noon and night, gave some to friends, and still had plenty left for Mom to make into jam.

Each year, before the first frost, the shelves in the cellar were laden with a rainbow of Mason jars. Yellow peaches, red jams and jellies, green pickles, scarlet tomatoes, even brown beef glowed from within the glass containers in the stark light of the bare bulb that lighted the room. Through the long Wisconsin winter we emptied the jars one by one, washed them and put them back on the shelf to be filled again the next summer.

The original cellar was a rough, dark, gloomy place, with a dirt floor, low ceiling and walls of flagstones set irregularly in layers. Dad improved it somewhat in the early 1930's when he laid a concrete floor, painted the flagstone walls white and built a wall to provide a storage area in front and a furnace/laundry room in the back. A steep wooden stairway led down from the kitchen to the storage area where canned goods and potatoes were kept. A stairway of steep, uneven, rough-edged concrete steps came in from the outside. The top of this stairwell was covered by a wooden door to keep out the rain and a heavy wooden door at the bottom locked with a sliding bolt to secure the cellar from intruders. We didn't lock the upstairs doors when we went out, so we rarely bothered to bolt the cellar door, either.

In the fall we filled the potato bin, a wooden box about four feet by four feet, with potatoes dug from our garden. We ate potatoes twice a day through the winter but there were still plenty left in the spring. By then, some had sprouted and some had begun to rot. We picked them over, threw out the soft and rotted, and kept the largest and firmest for seed. We cut each seed potato into sections, making sure each section had an eye that would sprout, and planted them. By fall, each partial potato had grown into a plant that produced ten to fifteen potatoes, more than enough to fill the potato bin again.

There were no windows in the storage area, but the back room of the basement had three ground level windows that brightened the room a bit. Chunks of wood and later coal were unloaded into the basement through the window nearest the furnace. This was also the room where Mom did the laundry, using a Maytag wringer washing machine. Over sixty years of washing clothes, Mom only had two washing machines - both Maytags. The first, purchased in 1930, had a ten-gallon tub with a central agitator and swivel wringer on the top. When it wore out after 30 years she had hoped to replace it with an automatic, spin-dry washer, but our well pump and storage tank did not have the capacity or the pressure for a modern appliance. So she bought another Maytag, a bit more stylish and sleek, but not all that much different from the first. In 1997, when widening of Highway 14 forced her to move, her new house had the automatic, spin-dry washer she had hoped for thirty years before.

The truck I drove, loaded with hay

Dirt was part of farm life. Dust — from the gravel road, field work and animals — drifted in through the open windows of the house in summer, coating the furniture and settling in the rugs. In winter, dust from the furnace did the same. Farm work dirtied clothes quickly and thoroughly, summer and winter, making laundry day a full scale operation. One tub of hot water in the old washing machine served for all the clothes. White things — underwear, sheets and shirts — were washed first, run through the wringer into another tub of fresh water, rinsed, and run through the wringer again into a basket. Colored items were next and followed the same procedure. Last came our overalls. These turned the water a muddy gray as the agitator swirled them around in the soapy water. Mom carried each batch of clean clothes upstairs and hung them on the clothes line next to the house. In summer, the line of laundry seemed to sparkle as it dried in the gentle breeze. In winter, when the wind blew over snow-covered fields and the temperature was 20 degrees, the pieces of wet clothing began to freeze even as Mom draped them over the metal wire which served as the clothes line. Her gloves turned to ice and her fingers grew numb before she had pinned the load in place. In the afternoon, she removed the clothes from the line, stacked them, still frozen, in frigid piles, and took them to the basement to thaw and finally dry.

Our toilet, located about 25 feet from the house, was a classic three-hole outhouse. That was our only toilet until 1941, when Dad built a small closet in the basement and installed a toilet stool that used chemicals to prevent smells. With a toilet in the basement we no longer had to make frigid visits to the outhouse in subzero weather. I am sure Mom and Shirl were happiest about that. Dad and I usually utilized the privacy and warmth of the barn for our toilet needs in winter. Dad even kept a roll of toilet paper hanging on the wall in the barn. When nature called he squatted over the gutter at the end of the barn. Even when we had indoor plumbing, he continued to use the barn. A trip to the house to sit on a fancy seat with running water would have carried in dirt and wasted time. He began to use the indoor toilet regularly only after he retired.

Grandpa Fanning's threshing machine

Before Dad installed a pressure tank and piping to bring running water to the house, we washed in rainwater and carried well water for drinking. Rainwater collected in a brick-lined cistern on the side of the house and we used a pump by the kitchen sink to bring it up for washing. For our weekly bath in summer we took turns splashing in a tub of warm water in the entryway. In winter, we stoked up the cook stove and set the tub close to the open oven door. Even when the stove was blazing, bathing in the kitchen was a chilly, uncomfortable experience and we hurried through it as quickly as possible.

I was fourteen in 1946, ready to enter high school, when Dad installed hot and cold running water in our house. He used part of the front porch to build a small bathroom with a sink and bathtub. What a luxury it was for me to fill the new tub with hot water and immerse myself in it, and for Mom to simply turn a faucet and have hot water to wash the dishes! We removed the water bucket and chipped dipper from behind the stove and sent the hand pump by the sink to the dump. Dad broke up the outhouse and filled the hole with dirt. Only the sidewalk remained as a reminder of frigid visits on cold winter days.

Chapter 4

Field Work

One hundred and sixty acres, a dairy herd of 24 cows and a batch of pigs and chickens didn't provide us with a lot of money, but we worked hard and lived pretty well. Our work year started in the spring, when the warming sun renewed our spirits after a long Wisconsin winter. Our farm was divided into eight fields of about 15 acres each, and 40 additional acres left as woods, where the cows grazed in summer and we cut wood in winter. Corn, oats and hay were rotated on the eight fields and over time Dad tried tobacco, peas, hemp, sorghum and sugar beets as cash crops, never making a lot of money on any of them.

We were on the land as soon as the frost was out of the ground, usually mid- March, when the temperature was barely above freezing and a cold north wind was still blowing. We rode the tractor from morning till dusk, readying the fields for planting, hurrying to get the seeds in the ground so the kernels would have the full effect of the warming air.

As soon as I could walk I began to follow Dad around, standing in the barn while he harnessed the horses or readied the tractor, tagging along as he hooked them to the plow or corn planter, or watching — hoping to be asked to help — while he repaired a piece of machinery. When Dad was working in the field I carried his bag lunch and a Mason jar of water out to him. We sat together in the shade of a tree while he ate. Then he mounted the tractor again and set off across the field while I walked home with the bag and empty jar. In the evening I helped herd the cows into the barn and chased them out the door when milking was over. I watched and learned and waited till I could be part of the daily routine.

I didn't have to wait long. On a farm, an extra set of hands, no matter how small, is always welcome, and Dad soon found use for me. "Bob, I need some help here. Slide this bolt into the hole when I get this piece of metal lined up." "Rain's coming. We'd better get these chickens inside." "When you go get the cows, see if you can find that new calf in the woods." Soon Dad was giving me more and more duties.

"Here's how to put the milking machine together. From now on you can get it ready when you get home from school;" then, "When you get home from school, throw down the silage and give each cow a forkful;" and finally, "Bob, I'm going to finish plowing this field so get the cows in and start the milking."

When I was about eleven, tall enough to reach the brake pedals and strong enough to turn the steering wheel (there was no power steering), Dad put me on the tractor and sent me out to disk and drag the fields. The disk - a double row of beveled steel plates mounted vertically on turning axles - was used to cut last year's tangled cornstalks into pieces so they would not bunch up and clog the plow. After plowing, the land was disked again to break up big lumps of earth. Sometimes we pulled a drag — 5 or 6 rows of steel teeth mounted in parallel boards — behind the disk to crush the clods to a uniform smoothness. Disking and dragging were beginner jobs; straight lines and precision weren't required.

A Farmall F-12 tractor like the one I first learned to drive

Baling hay in the field

Dad rode a round or two with me to be sure I had everything under control, then said, "You're doing OK. Make sure
you don't miss any places. Come back to the barn when
you're finished," then jumped down from the tractor and
walked away. I was excited and elated to be on my own in the
field doing man's work. It was fun but after a couple of
hours the roaring engine had dulled my brain, dust coated
my clothes and clogged my nostrils, and my butt ached from
the metal seat. I could overlook those discomforts when I
reminded myself I was on my own. I could take a break
whenever I wanted — stop to look for berries in the fence
row, throw lumps of dirt at a crow or just walk around the
tractor to stretch my legs.

In March, when the sky was overcast and the cold wind
worked its way through my layers of clothing, each round
seemed to take longer than the last. But by April the breezes
were warm, the sky was clear, and wild flowers brightened
the fence rows. I took off my winter gear and soaked up the
sunshine. It was still dusty and the tractor seat just as uncomfortable, but I was happy to be roaring around on the tractor, preparing fields of rugged stubble for a new crop.

I didn't have a watch, so I estimated time by the sun and
my growing hunger. When my stomach began to growl, I
looked toward the house, hoping to see a wave from Dad,
the signal to come in for dinner. As I parked the tractor, he
usually walked over to see if I had had any problems. "How's
it going?" he would ask as I jumped down. "Everything
working all right? When you finish that field you can go up
by the pond and start disking." I brushed off an outer layer
of dust as I walked to the house to wash up. If there was
conversation over dinner it was about work to be done in the
afternoon. After we ate, I read a comic book on the porch

until Dad said, "You better get started if you want to finish that field today." This was not a suggestion, so I put down the book, donned my cap, checked the oil, filled the gas tank, started the tractor and headed back to the field.

The first tractor I drove was a Farmall F-12, a simple, basic, rather ugly machine that had a top speed of five miles an hour. The metal seat, mounted on a vertical steel rod welded to the tractor frame, transferred every bump and jolt straight up to my tailbone. The notched throttle rod was set so far off on the left side that I sometimes slipped off the seat trying to set it. The steering wheel was small and mounted straight up-and-down, making it hard to turn. Fumes spewed directly into the driver's face from the exhaust pipe. Worst of all, the F-12 had no starter. In summer, one good turn on the crank could get the engine roaring, but on cold or damp mornings, a half hour of cranking might bring only a sore arm and muttered curses from Dad as he checked the magneto, gas lines, carburetor settings and throttle to try to find out why it wouldn't start.

Early engines were as temperamental as horses and everyone had a story of fractured wrists, broken thumbs and cracked skulls from backfires or slipped cranks. Dad wore a cast for a while after a Model-T Ford kicked back and broke his wrist, and our neighbor was injured when the crank flew off the crankshaft of the tractor he was trying to start and hit him in the forehead. The next day Dad wired the crank to the crankshaft of our tractor so it couldn't come off. I did a lot of cranking before we got a tractor with a starter. Though I survived without a broken bone or cracked skull, I never lost the fear that rose each time I grasped the crank handle.

I soon moved up from disking to plowing, steering a straight line across the field and keeping the rear tire of the tractor close to the edge of the furrow so the three plow lays caught and turned as much soil as possible. The challenge came as I approached the fence at the end of the field. I spun the turning knob on the steering wheel with my left hand while jerking the trip rope with my right to bring the plow out of the ground. Completing the turn, aligning again with the furrow, I pulled the rope to drop the plow into the ground and then settled down to the boring ride across the field. As I gained confidence I tried to make the turn a little faster and a little closer to the fence each time, a small competition with myself that speeded the job and broke the tedium of the long trek across the field.

It wasn't all tedium. On warm days, when the air was still and the ground dry, it gave me a good feeling to watch the plow shares cutting through the brown stubble, turning over the rich black soil, filling the air with the musty odor of humus. Blackbirds, killdeer, robins and sparrows flew in to feast on worms and grubs that suddenly found themselves on the surface. On days like that I thought it would be hard to improve on the life of a farmer.

Our farm was on the edge of the prairie. A layer of black topsoil a foot thick lay everywhere but on the gravel knoll just below our woods. There the soil was a sandy, gravely loam, probably deposited by the last glacier of the Ice Age. It was a difficult field to work because large rocks were hidden in the sandy soil, moving closer to the surface with each freeze and thaw. I only learned their location when the plow jerked sideways, sparks flew, and, sometimes, the tip of the plowshare broke off. Some areas on top of the knoll were so infertile and rocky that we just raised the plow out of the ground rather than risk a trip to the blacksmith. Plants never grew to any size there anyway.

Dad bought a bright orange Allis Chalmers tractor in 1944 or 1945. It was a few years old when we got it, but we never bought anything new except clothes. The Allis had four gears, a speed of 15 mph on the road, a starter, headlights, the throttle on the steering column, hand and foot brakes, and a coiled spring seat that absorbed the jolts and bounces. For cold weather work Dad installed a canvas cone that retained heat from the engine in a cockpit around the seat, making field work on windy days in March almost comfortable.

Not only was the new Allis faster, easier to start, and more comfortable than the F-12, it had a mechanism that used the forward motion of the tractor to elevate the corn cultivator. The cultivator shoes of the F-12 had to be lifted manually at the end of each row, an operation requiring strong arms and a firm grip. The Allis cultivator worked so well even a kid of twelve - like me - could operate it .

The arrow-shaped shoes of a cultivator dig up the ground on either side of a row of corn, rooting out weeds and building a protective mound of soil around the corn stalks. There was no danger of covering the plants when cultivating with a team of horses or the old F-12. With the Allis, on the other hand, I had to find an optimum speed. If I went too slow, I was wasting time; if I went too fast, I buried hills of corn. The right speed was important, and so was driving. If the tractor wandered even a foot off line, young plants would be dug up or covered with dirt. Dad made clear to me that covering even one hill of corn was a loss, so I kept the speed under control and watched both where I was going and where I had been. If I saw that I had covered a plant, I stopped, got down, walked back and cleared the dirt away by hand. Cultivating was serious business and I tried to do a good job. Years later

Mom told me Dad had remarked, "Bob can cultivate more corn in a day than anyone I've ever seen." (He never told me though, thinking, I guess, that such praise would go to my head.)

I could do all the field jobs — except planting. Dad did the planting. This job had to be done meticulously, in straight rows, checking regularly to be sure the planter had not plugged up, that seeds and fertilizer were being dropped in proper proportions. Dad often stopped and walked back a few yards to dig in the soil with his finger to be sure seeds were there. Planting was one job I never thought he might some day entrust to me.

Oats are fast growing and are planted in April. Seedlings peek above ground in a couple of weeks, and the crop was ready to harvest in late June or early July. A thunderstorm with strong winds near harvest time, when the stalks were top heavy with kernels, could flatten a field of grain, leaving a wet, tangled mess on the ground. If sunshine followed the rain the stalks dried out and righted themselves in a couple of days. If the sun didn't appear, the sodden kernels began to rot and the crop was lost. After every summer storm, we walked out to inspect the sodden, yellow pad of fallen oats, hoping we would see the sun the next day. Fortunately, Wisconsin storms are almost always followed by fair weather, reviving our crops.

Before the invention of the combine, threshing was a labor intensive and time consuming job. Ripe oats were cut and tied in bundles by a reaper not far advanced from the one McCormick invented in the 1860's. These bundles were stacked in the field in neat piles called shocks, left to dry for a few days, then loaded on a wagon, carried to the threshing machine and thrown, a bundle at a time, on a conveyor that carried it through a series of hammers, shakers and sieves that separated kernels from stalks. The grain was either bagged or run loose into a wagon box and the straw was blown out a large pipe to form a straw stack. Eight to ten men, four wagons and four teams of horses worked two to three long days to harvest our 30 acres of oats, breaking only at noon to troop to the house to enjoy the meal Mom had worked all morning to prepare.

In the early 1940's, Dad and his neighbors, Art Lucht and Mark Campbell, pooled their money and bought a used combine. It was a small machine but a major investment for the three farmers. Its cutting blade, run off the tractor's power takeoff, was barely six feet wide. The question was: could a combine be as efficient as the massive threshing machine? The first day, Dad walked behind the moving combine, checking the straw to see if the shakers had removed every kernel, examining the ground to see if kernels had been carried through the machine. Satisfied with his inspection, Dad pronounced the combine a timely replacement for the dust-raising noisy thresher and its legion of workers. From then on Dad ran the combine and I manned the truck, reading a book until Dad signaled that the grain hopper was full, then maneuvering the truck under the augur that unloaded the grain. When the truck was full, I drove to the granary to shovel off the load a scoop at a time. Some farmers had grain elevators that effortlessly carried the grain from the truck into the granary. But such technology came at a price, so we used muscle power to unload our grain. The straw that spewed from the back of the combine was baled and put in the barn to use as winter bedding for the cows.

Before and after harvesting oats we brought in the hay -

usually in May and late July. Two crops each summer filled the haymow with alfalfa and clover that fed our cattle and horses through the winter. Cutting and raking hay was Grandpa Knopes' job. We kept the mower and hay rake fitted for our team of horses, and Grandpa, in his 70s, was happy to sit on the backless metal seat, cutting and raking the hay. After cutting, the hay was left lying flat so it would begin to dry. Its fragrance could be smelled a mile away. The next day Grandpa raked it into windrows to speed drying. With a breeze and sunshine, hay would dry out in one day, but if there was any doubt, we waited. Every year we heard of barns lost to spontaneous combustion after damp hay had been put in the haymow. Dad was careful about checking the moisture content.

When the hay met the dryness test, we hooked the hay loader behind the wagon and started loading. Before we began to use the truck for hay, I stood at the front of the wagon, reins in hand, guiding the horses along the windrows while Dad caught the hay with a pitchfork as it came up on the loader, and spread it evenly over the wagon bed. The hay kept coming until Dad had built the load over my head and I stood in a cubbyhole of hay. The finished load was so high it brushed the electric wires as we drove across the yard to the barn.

A long rope and a series of pulleys were used to pull hay into the haymow. The team of horses or the tractor was hitched to one end of the rope, which was channeled through the hayloft, along a track under the roof and down to the wagon load of hay waiting to be unloaded. The hay fork, a four-pronged steel claw, was attached to the other end of the rope. Dad had set the fork deep in the load of hay, and yelled to the man (or woman, usually Mom) driving the horses or the tractor to begin the pull. As the horses moved away from the barn, the rope pulled the fork off the wagon and up to the roof of the barn where it locked on a set of wheels and was carried along a track into the haymow. When the forkload of hay reached the appropriate mow, the men in the barn yelled, "Drop it." Dad pulled on the trip rope and dumped the load into the haymow. The horses stopped and reversed direction, Dad pulled on the trip rope to bring the fork back down to the wagon, and the procedure started again. As Dad reset the fork, the men in the haymow spread the hay to the sides of the barn, stacking it higher and higher with each successive load until their heads were near the barn roof. This was a hot, dirty job, especially when the second crop of hay was harvested. There was no breeze in the haymow, and the temperature at times rose above 90 degrees in August. The men were soaked with perspiration and covered with dust as they pushed the loads around. Rinsing off at the pump and drinking a cool beer or soda after the last wagon was unloaded was a treat I still remember.

As I grew, I graduated from driving the tractor on the hay rope to handling the trip rope to stowing hay in the hayloft. One day Dad said, "Bob, you know how to set the fork. Go ahead and try a load." I had watched the procedure hundreds of times. I knew just how Dad positioned the fork and how he sometimes stood on the fork to keep it in place as the load began to lift, holding one of the ropes as it ran through the pulley for balance.

But, the first time I tried to use Dad's method of standing on the fork, I discovered I had missed something important. Dad had gripped the rope that was moving up, away from the pulley. I grasped the rope that was descending into the pulley and, before I could react, my fingers were jammed between the pulley and the rope and I was being carried upward with the forkload of hay. Mom, hearing my screams, stopped the tractor but didn't know which way to go. In a few seconds she understood what had happened and moved forward, but to me it seemed like hours before the fork landed again on the wagon bed, the rope slackened, and my fingers were free. I expected to see blood and broken bones, but my fingers had jammed the pulley and the rope had not moved. I had only bruises and another reminder that minor miscalculations on a farm can have serious consequences.

Working with loose hay was dirty, dusty and difficult and we were happy when hay balers were developed. A baler gathered hay from the windrow and used a powerful ram to compress it into a 60-pound bale. Two guys sat on either side of the machine, tying each bale together with two strands of baling wire. When I was in high school I worked on a baler for $5 a day — the grittiest, dirtiest, dustiest job I ever had. Bales were easier to work with than loose hay, they took up less room in the barn, and they could be retrieved easily in winter. In addition, baling wire became the Band-Aid of the farm. After we broke apart a bale we hung the wires on the wall of the barn and used them whenever there was something to repair, fasten, attach, secure, or generally hold together. We were disappointed when new balers were developed that used twine instead of wire. Twine balers tied the twine automatically and were operated by one man, and so were more efficient and economical than their predecessors. We had to admit that twine-bound bales were just as handy and serviceable as those tied with wire, but we knew that twine couldn't replace baling wire for all-around utility.

Dad has set the fork in a wagon load of hay bales
preparatory to sending them into the hay mow

Corn had a long growing season and was planted in rows about two-feet apart. Dad said that if the corn wasn't "knee high by the Fourth of July" the crop was behind schedule. If all went well, by September the corn I had cultivated as sprouts had grown seven-feet tall and was heavy with ripening ears. Some of this corn we used to make silage to feed the cows through the winter. The rest was left in the field so the ears would dry on the stalks, then picked and put in the corncrib and used for cattle and pig feed.

To make silage, the corn binder cut the green corn off near the ground, gathered it into a bundle, tied it with twine, and dropped it on a conveyor that carried it up to the wagon. I drove the tractor while Dad loaded the bundles. One day

Dad said, "Bob, why don't you load this one?" Anxious to show how strong I had become, I jumped on the wagon and, as the bundles came up the conveyor, laid them cross-wise on the floor of the wagon, overlapping them to bind the load together, as I had seen Dad do. As I proudly drove the wagon I had loaded down the lane toward the barn I heard a soft, swishing sound behind me and looked around to see my load sliding softly off the wagon onto the ground. Aghast and embarrassed, I frantically started to reload the errant bundles before anyone saw what had happened. No such luck. Dad and Mark Campbell came down from the field to help me. "You'll do better next time," Dad said, meaning there would be no pause in my on-the-job-training.

We took the loads of corn to the silo next to the barn and unloaded into the silo filler. This was a simple machine, a metal conveyor that carried the bundles of corn to a set of blades spinning at tremendous speed. The blades cut the corn into one-inch pieces and blew them up 40 feet of pipe into the silo. As we threw the long bundles from the wagon onto the conveyor, they sometimes fell sideways, jamming the conveyor. Common sense and caution dictated that before reaching down to dislodge a jam, the conveyor should be stopped to avoid an accident. But there were many farm-ers who thought they couldn't spare the time to stop the machine, even for an instant, and paid for their impatience by losing a hand, or even an arm, a half inch at a time.

I discovered claustrophobia (though I didn't know the term at the time) when Dad said, "Bob, I need you to go up in the silo and move the blower hood around so it won't get plugged with silage." That sounded like a good job for a ten-year-old. We climbed up into the silo (a concrete cylin-der about fifteen-feet in diameter and 40 feet high) and I jumped through one of the square doors and scrambled up the growing pile of silage to grab the blower hood. Over the roar of the tractor and the blowing silage, Dad yelled, "Keep that hood moving so the silage falls level all around the silo." He then began to close the door I had come in, and those above, until only one, at the very top, was open. "Wait!" I wanted to yell, "Don't leave me here. What if something goes wrong and I get covered and suffocate?" But Dad was gone and I was alone, looking down the slope of silage and up at the last open door, well above my head. I felt a twinge of fear and began to pray that I would survive. The nuns taught me that prayers should be said with hands clasped in front and eyes raised to heaven. But I couldn't let go of the hood, so I held one hand in front of me in supplication and moved the hood around with the other. I don't know how long I was stranded in the silo but when I looked down I noticed that the silage was beginning to fill in the space below the doors. The distance to the open door was closing. Maybe I would not perish. Then, to my deep relief, Dad appeared in the open door, waved me over, reached down, and pulled me up and out. "It's getting late. Time to get the cows for milking," he said. "We'll finish filling tomorrow." The next day, I made sure I was not available to move the blower hood as the silage filled the silo to the roof.

In the 1940's, the corn binder went the way of the grain binder and the threshing machine, replaced by a chopper that cut up the corn in the field and blew the silage into an enclosed wagon that trailed behind. A conveyor in the bottom of the wagon carried the silage into the blower (silo filler minus cutting blades) which sent it up into the silo. Three men replaced a silo filling crew of eight, and not one had to touch a stalk of corn or risk a limb while freeing a jam of seven-foot bundles.

Mechanized corn pickers also came along, using large rollers to remove the dried ears of corn from the stalks right in the field and pulling off the husks in one operation. A two-row corn picker could roll through a 15-acre field of corn in a single day, whereas it had taken Dad almost a week to walk through the field, ripping off the ears one at a time, husking them, and throwing them into the horse-drawn wagon.

Over time, the steam engines, threshing machines, corn binders, silo fillers, and tractors we used became antiques, seen only in museums or rusting behind abandoned barns. Smoke-belching steam engines are the dinosaurs of the machine world, their giant fly wheels now used only to power machinery at thresherees (annual festivals displaying old farm machinery and equipment) and county fairs. Corn binders, corn pickers, hay rakes, drags and disks lacked the romance and character of steam engines and threshing machines, and disappeared into junkyards and landfills.

Chapter 5

School

*W*hen someone asks me where I went to school, it isn't high school or college that comes to my mind; my first thought is "Dillenbeck," the red brick school house where I learned to read and write. I wanted to start school when I was five and pestered Mom through the summer to take me up to Dillenbeck, certain they would not refuse a promising student like me. As we stood in the hall, me with a lunch pail in hand, the teacher explained to Mom that, to enter first grade, a child had to be six years old. I would have to wait until the following September. Mom had told me this many times over the summer, but I insisted that an exception would be made. Now it seemed I was not as special as I had thought.

When September 1938 finally came, I went happily up the road to Dillenbeck School and met the rest of the first-grade class — Bruce, Karl and Myron — with whom I would spend the next eight years quietly competing in class, in sports, and in games we played on weekend visits. One or two boys joined our class over the eight years, but they never stayed more than a year or two. We remained the Gang of Four — until a young lady named June joined us in fifth grade and stayed until we graduated. We had hoped to go through our final years at Dillenbeck as the four muske-teers. Now we were a mixed group, at least in name. I can't say we welcomed June, but we accepted her. And she accepted us. We worked together on class projects but she was not interested in our games or plans. Girls and boys organized separate activities, June made friends with girls of other classes, while in class we five worked our way toward graduation.

Dillenbeck School was built in the 1920's, one of the last of more than 6,000 country schools built to teach the Three R's — readin', 'ritin', and 'rithmetic — to Wisconsin farm kids. Ensuring that no one had to walk more than a mile to get this basic education, the State of Wisconsin built a wooden schoolhouse at almost every rural intersection: one room, one teacher, 15 to 25 students, and a potbellied stove for heat in winter. The schoolhouses were usually named for the nearest farm family - Mouat, Bevans, Huginin, Daisy Chapin - or identified by location - Six Corners, Five Points, Johnstown, or Rock Prairie.

One of the last country schools to be built, Dillenbeck was named for a pioneer Janesville family that had either moved on or died out. A small, overgrown cemetery not far from the school was the only reminder of their presence. Once protected by a wrought-iron fence, now rusted and broken, the cemetery still holds about ten gravestones — some broken, all askew — with dates of death in the 1860s and 1870s. Some were children, like Byron, just over seven years when he died in 1868, and Henry, perhaps his brother, whose stone says he died at 8 years and 5 months. Solomon, son of H.H. and C. Dillenbeck, died in 1861, age 19 years and 6 months. Zimmermans and Shewmakers are also buried there, their stones so weathered that dates or ages are illegible. It seems that Alonzo Zimmerman, who lived from 1832 to 1881, was the last entrant to this little plot, just

35 years before my grandfather bought our farm a mile away.

My school, named for those pioneer children who died young and probably never went to school, was not a traditional one-room wooden building. Although it started as a one-room school, it was built of brick, and soon expanded. When I attended it had two classrooms upstairs, and two activity rooms and a coal burning furnace in the basement. A four-by-six foot library with glass doors on the bookshelves housed our one-hundred-book collection. Behind the school were two white, wooden outhouses, boys' on the left, girls' on the right. A long-handled pump next to the school provided water for drinking and washing. One boy pumped while the others slurped the flowing water from cupped hands. For the girls there was a ceramic water fountain in the basement, filled each morning with a bucket of water carried from the pump — not an easy job in winter when the pump handle was coated with ice. There was no washroom. In warm weather, the boys rinsed off at the pump and wiped their hands on their overalls. The girls, I guess, didn't get dirty during the day.

In the early 1930's, at the beginning of the Great Depression, a settlement of small houses, shacks, and makeshift dwellings grew up on the edge of Janesville. This motley collection of residences, named the Boise Addition but known to nonresidents as "the Patch," sat just outside Janesville city limits, probably to benefit from lower county taxes. The family of one my classmates lived in a garage, with plans to build their house later; another lived in a house only partially completed, black insulation nailed in place on the outside with laths. His father hoped to add siding when times were better. Children from the Patch went to Dillenbeck rather than the nearby city school, and the one-room school built for farm kids in the 1920's had to add a second room to accommodate this unexpected influx. By the time I started first grade in 1938, Patch kids outnumbered farm kids ten to one. Dillenbeck had become a country school for city kids.

Grades one through four were set up in the new part of the school, which we called the "lower" or "little" room, referring to the size of the students, since both rooms were on the same level and the same size. Of course, the classroom for grades five through eight was known as the "upper" or "big" room. The classrooms were well lighted by a bank of windows that went almost to the top of the 16-foot ceilings. Blackboards lined the front wall and students' work was displayed on other walls. The iron frames of our desks were bolted to long strips of wood, so the whole row could be pushed aside for sweeping. Though fountain pens had replaced nib pens years before, our desks still had an inkwell in the corner. These had been dry for years, but the desktops were still patterned with splatters and drips from our predecessors and the desks were scarred with jackknife carvings made by farm boys who would rather have been home in the field. Under each desk top was a small storage space for books and papers, and maybe a snack, though we took a chance of losing that to a sharp-eyed teacher if we weren't careful when we snuck a bite during class. Each spring, when we cleaned out these cubby holes, we found missing homework, undelivered notes to the teacher and sometimes a forgotten candy bar wedged far in the back.

While I was still in the little room, our rows of 19th-century desks were replaced with individual desks resting on four legs, each with a swivel seat and a Formica top that could not be scarred, stained, or carved. Lifting the top revealed a storage space for all our school supplies and more. Best of all, the lifted lid screened us from the teacher for a quick bite of a candy bar or a whispered conversation. Of course, if the lid stayed open for very long, the teacher was sure to walk over to see what was going on.

Through all eight grades, I was the only farm kid in my class. Myron, Bruce and Karl all lived in the Patch, city kids who headed down the road together, away from me, after school. I envied them as I walked home alone, evening chores waiting for me. I imagined them planning games before dinner or working together on our homework assignment. Though I know now, and probably suspected then, that the space, freedom and responsibilities that came with life on the farm were more interesting and challenging than an occasional game after school, I always thought I was missing out on something.

Except when it was raining or snowing, I walked or rode my bike the mile and a quarter to school. In spring, freshly tilled fields were turning from brown to green as corn and oats sprouts poked through, and the rising sun warmed my back as I walked out our driveway and turned west, my shadow stretching far ahead of me on the light-colored gravel. Birds sang along the fence rows, cattle lowed as they headed to pasture, tractors growled and horses, already at work in the field, shook their harnesses. In the fall, grain stubble and ripening corn glowed gold in the sun and I craned my neck to watch long V's of ducks and geese flying south. In winter the sunlight was flat and feeble, giving no warmth. I walked in near silence as the birds kept their songs to themselves, and farm animals stood warm in the barns. I heard only the crunch of snow and ice under my boots as I marched between banks of snow piled eight feet high by the county snowplows.

Though my walks to and from school were solitary, they were not boring. Along the way I checked the farmyards of our neighbors - the Luchts, Campbells and Suttons - to see what was happening, stopped to see a swarm of bees explore a patch of spring flowers, watched a flock of birds scavenge for worms in a plowed field, or followed the lazy circling of a hawk high in the sky. I chucked stones at gophers as they ran for their holes or tried to catch a garter snake as it wriggled across the gravel and into the grass. In winter I climbed the frozen cliffs of snow and ice left by snowplows, pretending I was on an Arctic expedition. When the temperature was in the teens and the sun low in the sky, the cold worked its way through my boots and mittens and I didn't have to imagine what the Arctic might be like. On those frigid days my fingers and toes were numb when I reached home and I ran to sit in front of the open oven door to warm up.

In winter I sometimes stopped at the greenhouse not far from school to warm up and watch the brightly colored parrot who sat on a perch in the office. "The parrot bites," the owner always warned. "Don't get too close." But when the owner wasn't around I edged a little nearer to the perch, till one day the parrot stretched out his neck, sank his sharp beak into my bicep and removed a small triangle of my skin through three layers of winter clothing. As I yelped in pain and jumped away, the parrot hopped back on his perch with a loud squawk that sounded like a laugh to me.

Across the road from the greenhouse was Archie Woodman's farm. Mr. Woodman was a friend of Dad's. One day he motioned me in to show me a porcupine he had trapped up north. He kept it in an old water tank by his barn and the animal's long hard quills made a rasping sound as they brushed against the metal side of the tank. I didn't have to be warned about the quills; I could see they could do serious harm if I got too near. It was certainly the most unusual animal I had ever seen, but the longer I watched the more I pitied the lonely creature as it explored the tank, looking for an exit. I didn't stop again to see the porcupine and I hoped Mr. Woodman took it back up north and turned it loose while it was still healthy.

By the 1930s, most farm homes had a telephone, but schools did not. The teacher communicated with parents by sending notes about absences, sickness, or special needs home with a child. If parents wanted to talk with a teacher, they came in person, and if a child became sick or injured the teacher loaded the student in her car and returned him or her to the jurisdiction of the parents. During school hours, the teacher was in charge, backed up by parents and the school board with the authority to use discipline as they saw fit.

On a cold fall day in third grade, I got a taste of just how much authority my teacher had. It was raining hard, so we were sent to the basement activity room with the admonition, "Stay away from the water that is seeping in by the rear door!" Of course, to third graders that's almost an invitation and, sure enough, we were slopping around in that water when our teacher came down waving a foot-long, steel-edged ruler. "I told you not to go near that water," she reminded us. "Get upstairs this instant!" As we passed her at the door, she gave each of us a solid whack with the ruler. To soften the blow I put my hands behind me and caught the edge of the ruler solidly on my palms. When I got home I showed Mom my still-red hands and complained that the teacher had hit me with a ruler. "You probably deserved it," Mom said, succinctly clarifying the rules. The teacher was there to teach. I was there to learn. If a swat on the bottom helped me to pay attention to instructions, so be it. That's how it worked at home, that's how it worked at school, and I expected it would probably work that way when I finished school.

Corporal punishment was not common at Dillenbeck. Except for an occasional grip of an arm or pull on an ear, I didn't receive another blow from a teacher after the ruler incident. Looking back, I think that swat on my bottom was the over-reaction of a new teacher. Persistent troublemakers and the insolent were sent home until the culprit's parents brought him (it was always a boy) back to apologize, but expulsion was rare. Punishment was usually a lecture from the teacher, isolation in the classroom, or extra homework. Parents knew the value of education and expected their children to be serious about learning and respectful to the teacher.

Even those who had been punished for their acts or attitude did not bear a grudge. One of my teachers, an avid bowler, often told us about her weekly games with a teachers' league. One morning she related to us the part she played in her team's victory the previous evening. In her final frame she needed a strike, and was disappointed when one pin still stood solidly after nine had fallen. Suddenly the lone pin toppled over. She looked down the alley and when she saw the pin boy smile and give a slight wave of recognition, she recognized him as a recent Dillenbeck graduate, a boy she had frequently disciplined. She realized he had just given her a small graduation present.

Eighth grade class - Dillenbeck School - 1946
l-r Myron Parsons, Karl Thom, Bob Knopes, Mrs. Hallenbeck,
June McNamee, Bruce Steinmetz

Discipline was important when one teacher was solely responsible for managing and teaching thirty or more students. Through the day, the four grades took turns sitting in the chairs next to the teacher's desk reciting lessons, each grade and each subject receiving equal time. As one class finished, the teacher would say, "It's now time for third grade arithmetic" or "Fourth grade social studies, please come up." The other three classes remained at their desks, reading or working on assigned projects, though some slipped comic books inside a textbook, carried on whispered conversations or passed notes. It was something of a game — the teacher listening to recitations while at the same time surveying the room to see if anyone was misbehaving, the sitting students watching the teacher to see what they might get away with. There were lapses, of course, like when a student became so absorbed in a contraband comic book that he didn't notice the teacher rise from her desk and move silently on crepe-soled shoes to his desk to confiscate the book. Or when the teacher became so involved with the class by her desk that she didn't notice the boy in the back row slide from his seat and slither out the door for an unapproved toilet break.

There were unanticipated disruptions, like the embarrassing time I literally lost my marbles in front of the class. In winter we were allowed to mark a circle on the classroom floor and shoot marbles at lunch hour. Between games I stored my marbles in the upper front pocket of my bib overalls. When I bent over to pick up a book, some marbles rolled out of my pocket, and bounced on the floor. I quickly straightened up and grabbed the pocket but loose marbles slipped down my chest and fell from the bottom of the sweater I wore over my overalls. I bent over to retrieve those, and more rolled out of my upper pocket. The clacking marbles got the attention of the room and my frantic up and down struggle to stop their escape had everyone, even the teacher, laughing.

Occasionally an art instructor from the county education office visited our classroom to give basic lessons in drawing. For a brief period, our school was even part of a "distance learning" (as it's called now) experiment. Hoping to broaden the curriculum, and perhaps take some of the load off country school teachers, the county installed a loud speaker to beam weekly lessons on various subjects into our classroom. We waited in anticipation for the first lecture and, at the appointed hour, our teacher turned on the speaker and adjusted the the volume. Through intermittent static we heard a faint voice but could make out only part of what was being said. Increasing the volume only made the static louder. The voice faded in and out, our teacher grew perturbed and the students, not used to passive listening, began to fidget, whisper and poke one another. We tried again the next week, with the same result. After that, the speaker sat silent on the shelf over our heads and we went back to our normal routine.

Of the three teachers I had during eight years at Dillenbeck, Mrs. Hallenbeck, my mentor in grades 5 through 8, was the most memorable. Tough but understanding, she was totally committed to her career and her students. She did whatever needed to be done at school, including stoking the furnace and cleaning up when the parent who had volunteered to do the job was late or forgot. She stayed late after school working on lesson plans and worksheets, and spent hours running off assignments on a primitive copier called a hectograph — making a master copy, transferring it to gelatinous plates with a special fluid, then making copies, one sheet of paper at a time. Christmas and graduation programs were minor extravaganzas with every student playing a part and having a job to do. No detail and no student was overlooked. Mrs. Hallenbeck wrote the skits and speeches, made the decorations, sent out the invitations, and made sure we cleaned up afterwards. In the spring she asked her students to bring rakes and clippers to school on Saturday morning so we could clean up the campus. One year she recruited Dad to bring a truckload of large stones to build a border along the circular driveway. Almost every student showed up for these cleanups and worked until the school yard was neat and orderly. Though it wasn't part of the curriculum, we learned duty, loyalty, and commitment from Mrs. Hallenbeck.

With an eighth grade education and a certificate from Janesville Normal School, Olive Hallenbeck began teaching at age 17. Her first teaching job was in a ramshackle one-room school south of Janesville, where she said she stuffed pieces of paper and cloth into crevices in the walls to keep out the winter wind. Over the next 50 years she taught in schools named Johnstown, Creekside, Townline, Gravel Hill, Burdick, Frances Willard, and Powers, ending her county career as principal of Dillenbeck and Consolidated schools. When she reached Rock County's mandatory retirement age, she moved to St. Mary's Parochial School, which had no age limitation, and taught for ten more years.

When I was in eighth grade, Mrs. Hallenbeck offered to pay me ten cents a day to stay after school and help her clean up. Fifty cents a week was a lot of money to me, so I accepted her offer and each afternoon gathered the cloth blackboard erasers, took them outside, and clapped them against the brick wall until they were free of chalk. Then I pumped a bucket of water at the well and wiped clean all the blackboards. On Friday afternoon I swept the floors. I don't know why Mrs. Hallenbeck offered me the job. Maybe she had grown tired of asking for volunteers or of doing these jobs herself (she paid me from her own funds). She might have wanted company in the empty building as she worked on lessons for the next day.

The county education office developed our curriculum to give a basic grounding in the Three R's, and expose us to a little art, culture, and science. From first through eighth grades our report cards listed the same subjects: spelling, reading, writing, arithmetic, language, geography, science, music and art. They were the same subjects, but each year our textbooks got a little thicker and the material more detailed. Writing class concentrated on rules, not composition. We started in first grade with two- and three-word sentences in a book about Dick and Jane and their dog Spot ("See Spot. See Spot run.") and learned phonics to sound out new words. By fifth grade we were conjugating verbs, learning the rules of grammar and parts of speech, and analyzing sentences, filling page after page with complicated diagrams of the part played by each word in a sentence. Writing class was penmanship. Our fingers cramped as we struggled to form letters of an exact size within measured lines, checking our progress by holding a Parker Method template over our work to see that each letter was perfect, not too large or too small, not leaning or tilting the wrong way. Though my penmanship was always haphazard and my lines never straight, I still know how to form a perfect letter, a useless but satisfying skill in today's world of e-mail and instant messaging.

In art class we pored over prints of paintings with agricultural themes: French peasants in a field at dusk in "The Angelus," "The Horse Fair" by Rosa Bonheur, or a portrait of a blacksmith, included, I suppose, because blacksmithing was still important to farmers. We were given art assignments, but when I tried my hand at drawing, my animals were unrecognizable, my people malformed and my scenes without perspective. Seeking another, and possibly more satisfying way to express myself, for one assignment I decided to carve a rabbit from a bar of soap. Holding the soap over a pan to catch the shavings, I began to whittle, expecting a shape to appear. As more and more shavings fell into the pan, it was clear that the rabbit, if it finally appeared, would be quite small. In the end, I had only a sliver of soap in my hand and a pile of shavings in the pan. I grabbed a pencil and paper and dashed off another of my skewed, distorted, clumsy pictures so I would have something to turn in the next day.

In geography class, we began with Rock County, studied Wisconsin land forms, and then considered the entire United States. World geography was an exercise in memorization until I became interested in what was happening on the battlefields of World War II. When the Japanese invaded the Philippines in December, 1941, we grimly read daily reports in the Janesville Gazette about the fighting on Bataan and the fall of Corregidor. We worried about friends and relatives who were stationed there with the Wisconsin National Guard and wondered how many had survived the Death March to Japanese prison camps. Only when survivors of the Janesville tank company returned after the war did we learn that two of Mom's cousins, Harold Fanning and Jim Manogue, had died of malaria in a Japanese prison camp in 1944.

As the tide of war turned I learned the names of island chains in the Pacific where American troops landed as they moved west toward Japan. In Europe I followed the Battle of Britain, D-Day landings in France in 1944, the Battle of the Bulge in Luxembourg — where my grandfather had been born — and the approaching end of the war as allied forces moved east across Europe to meet the Russian army at the Elbe River in 1945.

In 1942, our teachers took the entire student body out along nearby roads to collect pods from milkweed plants. We were told the fluffy white seeds in the pods would be used as filling for life jackets. We were proud to be part of the war effort, but I read no reports of milkweed-filled life jackets and there was no follow-up collection the next year. Still, science projects occasionally took us into nearby fields to collect flowers, leaves and seeds to identify, noting which were noxious weeds and which were decorative wild flowers. We also learned what fertilizers worked best on various types of soil and studied worms and insects that destroyed crops. I learned what to look for when Dad asked if I had seen signs of army worms or corn borers in the cornfield. This was practical science for the farm, but of little use and only passing interest to my urban classmates.

Mom packed a lunch for me every day: a sandwich, an apple and a store-bought dessert. At home we ate Mom's cookies, cakes, and pies, but for my school lunch I preferred a Twinkie or cream-filled chocolate. I also filled a glass-lined thermos with Koolaid and secured it in my lunch box with a metal clip. The thermos was fragile and shattered easily, even if dropped on grass. I tried to be careful, but I broke about one a month. If I dropped my lunch box on the way to school, the Koolaid soaked my sandwiches. If it happened on the way home I took out the thermos and shook it, hoping I would not hear the rattle of broken glass. It usually broke, and I always got a lecture on responsibility and thrift, ending with a reminder that new liners cost thirty cents each.

In good weather we ate our lunches outside under a tree. In winter and on rainy days we ate at our desks. If hunger struck midmorning, we asked permission to go out to the toilet and grabbed a snack from our lunch bucket as we passed through the cloakroom.

Playground equipment at our school was basic and simple: a set of swings, a slide, and a merry-go-round for the girls and the little kids; a football, a soccer ball, a softball and two bats for the boys. Everyone liked the merry-go-round. Younger kids held tight to the safety bar as bigger boys held the vertical poles and ran as fast as they could to get the ride spinning. Some thought it fun to rock the merry-go-round from side to side, but the ride was not designed to handle sideways movement and, sooner or later, the welded joints cracked and the platform collapsed. This irritated the school board and if it happened more than once in a school year, they refused to pay for repairs and the merry-go-round sat lopsided and unused for months.

Though I never lacked for entertainment on my way to school, I quickened my pace when I got close to the school yard and heard a game in progress. In the fall the boys played football or soccer; in the spring, softball. The girls contented themselves with the swings, jacks, jump rope and hop scotch. Our playing field was more than an acre, long but not too wide, fine for football and soccer, but chancy for softball. A hit to left field easily carried over the woven wire fence — topped by two strands of barbed wire — that separated the school yard from Mr. Woodman's pasture. This was a home run, of course, but we had only one ball. It had to be retrieved or the game was over. We helped one of the younger, faster kids over the fence, then kept an eye on the grazing cattle as he made a dash for the ball, ready to alert him if one of the placid grazers in the pasture turned out to be a bull. We never lost a player or a ball, but every time Archie Woodman saw one of us climb his fence, he came running, threatening to whip us all if we bothered his cows again.

The school year closed with Rock County Play Day, when students and teachers of county schools gathered for a day of games and a picnic at Riverside Park in Janesville. There was a game for every age. The youngest children competed in the bean bag toss, foot races, and the softball throw (separate competition for girls and boys), while older kids had teams for volleyball, horseshoes, and softball. Losing was no disgrace, though every team and school wanted to do well. There were no prizes or awards beyond the joy of the moment. Though indifferent to our games during the year, Mrs. Hallenbeck tried to fire us up so we would be ready for Play Day. She made bean bags and coached the younger kids on how to throw them. She forced the tallest boys to join the girls to make up a volleyball team, a game most boys considered too tame during the year.

The game of softball played at Dillenbeck, and at most schools in our area, was sedate and relaxed, favoring the batter. Easy pitching allowed frequent fly balls that kept outfielders from getting bored and spared infielders the sting of stopping sharply hit grounders with their bare hands. We had a ball and two bats, but no mitts. At our last Play Day we faced a pitcher who ignored tradition, whipping the ball to the plate with tremendous speed. Even when we realized that few of his pitches were in the strike zone, we couldn't keep our bats still. One after another, he struck us out. "Don't swing," our team yelled from the bench. But when we went to the plate we were determined to show that pitcher he was not invincible. The harder we tried, the faster we went down. Had we stood, bats on our shoulders, never taking a swing, he would probably have walked us all. But we kept swinging, the umpire called strikes, and we lost by a large margin. It was an ignominious end to my grade school softball career, but the disappointment and embarrassment were forgotten as we prepared for graduation and high school in the fall.

Chapter 6

Entertainment

*B*efore I was big enough to help Dad with the milking machines, I went into the haymow each evening to throw down hay and straw for the animals. When I started this job, the hay lay loose, filling the barn to the rafters 25-feet above. Separating and pushing it down the chutes was a tough job. The job became easier after we began to bale hay — and more fun, too, as I climbed to the top of the mountain of bales, threw bales down to the floor, pushed them down the chute, cut the baling wire, and slid the slabs of hay into the mangers.

My work was always done before Dad finished milking and we had a little ritual. I would casually ask, "What time is it?" Dad would pull his watch from the top pocket of his bib overalls and say, " Almost seven. What's on tonight?" I had the weekly radio schedule memorized and my answer depended on the day of the week. If it was Monday, it was *Red Skelton*, on Tuesday, *The Lone Ranger*, and so on. "OK," Dad would say. "Go ahead in. We're about finished here." I would run into the house, straight to the big wooden radio with carved legs and scrollwork that was as tall as I, flick on the toggle switch, and tune the dial. I had to sit very close to the radio's speaker. My favorite programs came from Chicago stations and their signals were never strong. I could tell when a thunderstorm was coming by the amount of static on our radio. If a storm was nearby, we got no reception at all and I had to find another way to pass the evening.

Radio was my primary entertainment, my chance to enjoy a vicarious life away from the farm for a time. In the afternoon when I got home from school, I tuned to the fifteen-minute adventure series — *Captain Midnight, Jack Armstrong, the All-american Boy, Don Winslow of the Navy* — designed to sell Ovaltine and General Mills cereals to preteen boys. In the evening I listened to half-hour comedy shows like *Fibber McGee and Molly* and *The Great Gildersleeve*, adventure programs such as *The Shadow* or *Mr. District Attorney*, and variety shows like *Kay Kyser's College of Musical Knowledge*. When I was able convince Mom that I just couldn't miss a special program, she let me take my dinner plate from the table and eat by the radio.

Someone once said that radio is preferable to television because the pictures are better on radio. I know what he meant. Good radio conjures up images which are more vivid than TV can show, especially in the minds of children. As I listened to radio programs I could see the snakes and panthers in the Amazon jungle where Jack Armstrong was having his latest adventure; I saw Buck Rogers' spaceship and the aliens he encountered; and I pictured the streets, buildings and people in Times Square and the Chicago Loop when I listened to dramas on *The Lux Radio Theater* or *Twentieth Century Limited*. With my ear pressed against the speaker, I dreamed of a life in a big city that did not involve milking cows, carrying wood or riding a tractor around a dusty field.

Radio was also my introduction to music. On Saturday evening I learned the top ten songs of the week from *Your Hit Parade* and sang them on the tractor during the week. I heard dance bands aired live from hotel ballrooms in Chicago and New York. When a friend of the family offered us an ancient windup Victrola, I hounded Dad until he went to pick it up. After we set it up in the dining room, I found a pack of needles and a 78-rpm record in a drawer. I opened the wooden lid, put the record on the turntable, inserted a new needle, cranked the handle to wind the spring, and stated the turntable. Even though the sound was tinny and scratchy, I was thrilled to hear the music coming out of the single built-in speaker. The important thing was that I could hear music any time I wanted. From then on I was constantly after Mom to buy new records and needles, but the vinyl disks cost more than fifty cents cents each, so our collection grew slowly. Needles, too, cost money. They were sharp, but not very durable. If used for more than three or four playings, a needle would quickly wear down the grooves on the record.

Most Saturday evenings in summer we went to Milton Junction to sit on blankets in the park and watch grainy black-and-white movies projected on a large sheet suspended between two trees. Families and friends arranged their blankets near each other so children could play and women chat. The projectionist usually started the program before dusk, when there was still enough light in the sky to wash out the first fifteen minutes of action. But the kids sat down and became quiet as soon as the movie began, the women lowered their voices, and the men, one by one, drifted over to one of the two bars to drink beer and talk farming. We met at the car when the movie was over.

The program always opened with an installment of a serial adventure, followed by a cartoon, then the feature. The serial showed the hero escaping from the predicament he had fallen into the previous week, then got him into another situation just as the film was ending. It was up to the kids to make sure their parents brought them back to the park the next week to see how he got out of his latest jam. The feature was always a western, starring cowboys we didn't know and would never hear of again. The cowboy stars of the day — Tom Mix, Gene Autry, Hopalong Cassidy and the Cisco Kid — could be seen at either the Apollo or Beverly theater in Janesville, where tickets cost a dime, so no one complained about the quality of the films or the caliber of the actors in the free movies at the park. Two upscale theaters in town, the Jeffris and Myers, catered to high school age and older clientele and showed double features of first-run Hollywood movies.

Other than radio there were few diversions for a kid on a farm in the 1930's. I was always happy when a traveling salesmen showed up: the Watkins man with a trunk full of spices, extracts and cooking utensils for Mom to look over; a seller of bibles and religious paraphernalia; a traveling photographer who took pictures of Shirl and me posed on the piano bench; a representative of a feed company offering Dad the latest fertilizers and hybrid seed corn; or even the guy who collected dead animals who dropped in to see if we had a sick cow or recently deceased pig.

Then there was Doc Fesler, our veterinarian, who always brought a little comic relief to our daily routine when he came to treat a sick animal. He gave a yell of hello when he climbed out of his car and kept up a steady patter of conversation and nonsense as he checked over the patient. When he decided on treatment, he rummaged through the trunk of his car, inspecting then throwing aside boxes and bottles of medicine, salves, pills and powders until he found what he needed. He continued to comment and crack jokes as he smoothly jabbed a huge needle into a vein in the horse's neck for a blood sample or massaged a giant pill down the throat of a sick cow. I never volunteered, but Doc often put me to work holding the halter rope as he worked on an animal. One time he had me pulling on the hoof of a breech-birth calf as he and Dad worked to pull it from the womb of a struggling heifer. Doc was a veterinarian of the old school and his treatments were not always orthodox. Once, after cleaning a gaping chest wound on a horse that had run through a barbed wire fence, he got some black gunpowder from his trunk, saying, "This will heal him up fast," as he sprinkled it in the wound. The horse recovered nicely, although I doubt this treatment was taught in veterinarian schools.

Dad was never too busy to take a break and share a beer with a visitor, most of whom arrived with a six-pack in the car. If someone dropped by empty-handed Dad would say, "Bob, run out to the milk house and get a couple of beers." He always had a few bottles chilling in the cool water of the milk tank. I should have made a collection of the many types of bottles and cans we scattered along our fence rows over the years. When I was small, I collected the tall empty bottles and put them back in the wooden or heavy cardboard cases so Dad could take them back to the tavern to exchange for a fresh case. When throwaway bottles, and later tin cans, replaced returnable glass bottles, we flipped these over the nearest fence, to be gathered up in the spring and taken to the dump.

Friends who dropped by when Dad was in the field often pitched in to help and stayed for a few beers when the work was done. One bright fall day, after the last load of tobacco had been cut and hung in the tobacco shed, Orvis Reinhart, who frequently stopped by on his Harley-Davidson, suggested that Dad take his bike for a ride. Pleased at seeing the crop in the shed, perhaps taking the offer as a dare, Dad straddled the big machine, turned the throttle, and let out the clutch. The Harley leaped forward across the field, bouncing over mounds of dirt and stubs of tobacco plants. The wheels leapt unevenly from one row to the next, the front wheel hitting a bump as the rear wheel bounced off another. Dad had a firm grip on the handle bars but each time he hit the seat he bounced off again. His head was bobbing and his legs were flung out wide as he tried to keep his balance. It was a funny sight until we saw that he was heading for the wire fence. He got the machine under control before he reached the fence, turned it around, and slowly headed back, riding parallel to the rows. When he pulled up and parked, he said, "Damn, that was close. I didn't hit the seat long enough to reach the brake." To which Reinhart replied, "I should have told you there's a brake on the handle bars, too."

(That was the last time we saw Reinhart for a long time. He was a member of the Janesville National Guard — Company A of the 192nd Tank Battalion — which was activated in November 1940, and arrived in the Philippines mid-November 1941, less than a month before the Japanese invaded. The entire company was captured when Bataan fell in 1942. Of the 99 who left in 1941, only 35 returned in 1945, after four years in a Japanese prison camp. Reinhart was one of the 35, but I don't remember him coming out to our farm again after he got back.)

Beer was the drink of choice around a farm and, if I stood around long enough, Dad usually let me have a sip. I originally looked on beer as nothing more than a refreshing drink. But I changed my mind one spring when we went to help a neighbor strip tobacco. In March, when the air began to warm, it was time to strip the leaves from the tobacco stalks and bundle them for sale. The tobacco stalks were moved from the shed where they had hung over winter to a small room, where ten or twelve neighbors of all ages gathered around a wood-burning stove to talk as they stripped the leaves from the stalks. A pile of stalks was placed next to every chair and each person worked at his or her own pace. A man could pull off and hold in his hand the leaves from fifteen or more stalks before adding them to the paper-lined box in the center of the room. When the box was full, the bundle was tied with twine and stacked along the wall, ready for sale. The bare stalks were thrown aside and spread on the field as fertilizer for the next year.

A tub of cold drinks sat in the corner to quench the thirst raised by the odor and dust of wilted tobacco. No one noticed or cared when I took a beer and put it beside my chair. Through the evening I sipped beer and stripped tobacco. When I emptied one bottle, I took another. At the end of the evening I didn't feel very well. When I got up from the stool, my legs began to move in directions I did not want to go and my head began to spin. "How much beer did you have?" Mom asked as I made my unsteady way to the car. I had no idea, but I knew it had been too many. At home I struggled up the stairs to my bedroom, but as soon as I lay down the bed began spinning. As I sat on the edge of the bed waiting to see what would happen next, I swore that I would not touch another drop of beer for the rest of my life. This was the first of many such pledges over the years.

Chapter 7

On the Town

Saturday was the day Dad did the milking early, after which we piled into our 1932 Chevy sedan (we never had anything but a Chevy) and drove into Janesville to do our weekly shopping. Stores were open until 9 p.m. and farm families came from all directions to buy what they needed and to admire things they didn't need (and probably couldn't afford).

Our first stop was the grocery store. We parked at the rear door and Dad carried in eggs we had collected during the week. During the winter, when the hens were most productive, we filled two big crates each week, at least 50 dozen eggs. Mom gave her shopping list to the grocer to fill while his assistant "candled" our eggs, holding them up, one by one, in front of a light bulb to check for cracks in the shell, blood in the yolk or a developing chick. Our eggs were fresh from the nest and easily passed the test. Since the farm supplied most of our own needs, Mom's shopping list was not long. She bought staples, like breakfast cereal, flour, shortening and sugar for baking, coffee and tea, and things we couldn't grow ourselves, like oranges and bananas. As the grocer gathered Mom's order from barrels and shelves around the store, retrieving boxes from shelves up near the eleven-foot ceiling with a grappler on a long pole, Mom walked through the store to see if she had forgotten anything. When she was satisfied that she had everything she needed, our bill was toted up and reduced by the value of the eggs we had delivered. We loaded the groceries into our car, and set out for the stores on Main and Milwaukee streets. Main Street ran north and south, Milwaukee Street ran east and west and the intersection of the two was the shopping center of Janesville. All the stores that counted in Janesville were located on four blocks at the intersection of these two streets.

Clothing and department stores were mostly on Main Street, while national chain stores, like Sears & Roebuck, Kresge's, Woolworth's Five & Ten and Walgreen's, were on Milwaukee Street, across the bridge that spanned the Rock River. There was also a store that specialized in school supplies, a stationery store that shelved the latest hardcover books along with Bibles and prayer books, several shoe stores, two music stores, several jewelers, furniture stores, two hardware stores, two bakeries and plenty of banks and taverns. There was a fish market and a butcher shop on Milwaukee Street, though we rarely shopped at the fish market, put off by the smell and fear that fish bones might catch in our throat.

Parking was free in town, but finding a spot on Main Street on Saturday evening could be a problem, even though the police attempted to enforce a one-hour limit on parking space. A policeman rode along the main streets on a three-wheel motorcycle, making a mark on the rear tire of each parked vehicle with a piece of chalk on the end of a pole. If the mark was still there on his next pass, he wrote a parking ticket. It was an uncertain system. He might be back in an hour or he might not return at all. Always respectful of rules, Dad usually sat in the car with the motor running when his hour was up, ready to back out if the policeman returned. Being cautious was better than paying the city a dollar for a parking ticket. Parking meters were installed in Janesville in the 1960's — twelve minutes for a penny, an hour for a nickel — making it easier for a policeman to enforce the time limit, but antagonizing shoppers, who began to do their shopping at the new mall that had recently been built on Highway 26, not far from our farm.

Our second stop was one of the department stores that carried clothes for kids. I tried on shirts, pants, coats, and sweaters to wear to church and school until Mom and I agreed on fit, color and style. The clerk wrote up the bill, took the money from Mom, put it in a little container and pulled a cord, sending the container and our money singing up a system of wires to the cashier's office in the mezzanine at the back of the store. In a minute or two the little container came sailing back with a receipt and our change. I was willing to put up with the tedium of clothes shopping just to see those little containers of money flying around the store like frightened birds.

For everyday clothes, Dad and I went to Val Weber's little store on the outskirts of the shopping area, where farmers gathered in the fall to talk farming while picking out bib overalls, flannel shirts, heavy gloves, long underwear, and wool caps with ear flaps. In the spring they bought bib overalls, leather gloves, straw hats and blue work shirts. A pot-bellied stove warmed the store in winter, stoked so hot it singed the back of my wet glove one evening when I held it up to dry. Every fall Dad bought me a flat wool cap like the ones he had worn when he was young. I told him no one wore those caps anymore, but he was undeterred. He bought the cap. I wore it a few times, then buried it under gloves and mittens in the drawer by the kitchen door. The caps never appeared again so I suppose Mom passed them on to relatives or a charity.

After I was outfitted with new clothes, Dad usually gave me 10 or 15 cents and I would head up Milwaukee Street to check out the toy counter at Kresge's or Woolworth's. I walked along, looking at displays in store windows, jostled and pummeled by the crowd. I stopped to look down on the black and ominous darkness of the river as I crossed the Milwaukee Street bridge, then moved again into the brightness of store windows, street lamps and store signs. I looked over the toy trucks, guns and games, but often passed them by and settled for a Big Little Book, only four inches square but 100 pages thick. Each cost only a dime, and had an easy-to-read cowboy story. Best of all there were little pictures on the upper left hand corner of each page that became a short motion picture when I flipped the pages with my thumb.

I arranged to meet Dad at the Star Billiard parlor when the stores closed at nine. Star Billiard had a soda fountain with a long marble counter, a wall lined with the latest magazines and comic books, and rows of green-clad pool tables in the back room. I could hear the click of billiard balls as I ate a bowl of ice cream at the marble counter and sometimes peeked around the corner to watch the men as they played, moving around the big tables, muttering to themselves as they studied angles and chalked their cues. I bought my first comic books at the Star Billiard and expanded my horizons as I flipped through magazines on music and musicians, science, sports, and travel while waiting for Dad.

At the end of the evening, Dad and I walked through the thinning crowd to meet Mom at the car for the drive home. We slipped into the darkness of the countryside as we passed the last street light at the city limits, and I knew we were halfway home. I wouldn't see bright city lights again for another week.

Another diversion for me was riding with Dad to the feed mill in Milton Junction. When I saw him loading the truck with corn and oats, I stayed nearby so he wouldn't forget to say, "I'm going up to the Junction with this grist. Want to ride along, Bob?" Of course, I did. (I was always ready for a ride, even a short one on the running board of a car as it drove out our driveway. My aunt once discovered me sitting in the back seat of her car and put me out on the side of the road a half mile from home.)

Main street in Milton Junction was two blocks long, with railroad tracks running along one side, and a drug store, bank, clothing store, grocery store, barber, Chevrolet dealership and two taverns - the Spot and the Green Lantern - on the other. The feed mill was situated across the railroad tracks.

At the mill, Dad positioned the truck's front wheels on a metal frame, set the brake, and removed the truck's tailgate. The metal frame slowly lifted, raising the front end of the truck, spilling our load out the back and into a pit. The miller pushed a handle, an electric motor groaned to life, and I could hear grinding noises below us. We had to shout to be heard over the racket and our clothes were gradually covered with a fine powder that seemed to come from everywhere. In about fifteen minutes our load of oats and corn had been ground into feed, poured into gunny sacks and loaded on our truck. On top of the load Dad put a couple of blocks of salt and a bag of oyster shells. Cows need extra salt in the summer so we always put a block of salt in the pasture for them to lick. Oyster shells provide the calcium hens need to produce sturdy egg shells and we kept one feeder in the chicken house full of this supplement.

After the feed mill, we usually made a stop at the blacksmith shop. While the feed mill was a study in white, with a coating of pale dust covering everything, including the workers, the blacksmith shop was the polar opposite. From ceiling to floor, everything was coated with black soot, including the windows. And more dirt was generated all the time. A charcoal fire blazed red, always ready to heat chunks of metal, and sparks flew from grinding stones as metal was shaped and smoothed. A roaring diesel engine powered an array of drills, drop hammers, grinders, lathes, and saws through an intricate system of belts, pulleys, and gears. The welding machine blazed and crackled as new tips were fastened on plow shares and the air sizzled as an acetylene torch burned its way through pieces of metal. Dad warned me, "Don't look directly at the welder flame, it will ruin your eyes," and handed me a welder's helmet with a window of thick, dark glass so I could see what was going on. On some visits I stood by the blazing charcoal fire, my face burning, as the blacksmith removed a glowing piece of steel, laid it on an anvil and pounded it with a hammer until it was a perfect fit for a broken piece of equipment.

Before we headed for home we always made a stop at one of the two taverns, alternating, I suppose, so Dad didn't appear to favor one over the other. On a rainy day both would have a lively clientele of farmers who couldn't be in the field and didn't want to be in the barn. Even on fair days one or two locals would be on hand, leaning on the bar, talking to a farmer who was having a beer while waiting for the blacksmith to finish an emergency repair.

The Green Lantern was just a shack with a bar and a few

card tables. The Spot was in a two-story building that had once had a popular dance hall on the second floor. The owner had put off repairing the roof and before long leaks made the dance floor uneven and the upper level unusable. When rainwater gathered on the unused dance floor and began to run through into the tavern, the bartender solved the problem by drilling holes in the floor of the bar. A line of dilapidated, lopsided stools detracted from the luster of the long, polished wooden bar, but no one suggested they were inappropriate or should be replaced. During World War II, fading photos of the Axis leaders — Hitler, Mussolini, and Tojo — hung behind the bar, their faces framed in the three holes of a well-worn outhouse seat. It was a friendly place to spend time and, on a rainy day when there was no need to hurry home, Dad joined a euchre game at one of the tables while I drank 7-Up and played the skeet ball machine. Some farmers, usually the less successful ones, found it difficult to leave once the beer began to take effect and the card game became exciting, but Dad rarely stayed more than an hour. When he decided it was time to go he would say, "Well, drink up, boys," finish his glass of beer in two swallows, and be on his way out the door before anyone could say, "Wait a minute, Al, let me buy just one more." Caught by surprise, I often had to gulp down my 7-Up, and suffer a stomach ache on the way home.

When I was 11, Mom, hoping to broaden my social horizons, encouraged me to join the 4-H club, an organization for farm kids designed to teach setting goals, keeping records, and carrying through a project from idea to conclusion. The four H's stand for Head, Heart, Hands and Health, that is, thinking, commitment, work, and clean living. Each member was expected to take on one or more projects, like raising and training animals, gardening, handicrafts, sewing, and cooking. A project year ran from fall through the summer, culminating in the Rock County fair where projects were exhibited and judged.

Our 4-H club met once a month in the Harmony Town Hall, a one-room, clapboard-sided building that was also the meeting place of the town board, a voting precinct, and a venue for ice cream socials in summer. A potbellied stove in the middle of the room was the only heat in winter. As our meeting progressed on the cold winter nights, the entire club edged closer to this sole source of heat. Meetings opened with announcements and discussion of projects and ended with singing and games. Sometimes we opened the door of the stove to roast hot dogs and marshmallows.

When the Club sponsored dancing lessons one year, Mom insisted I participate. I signed up reluctantly and was surprised to see almost all club members show up at the first session. The instructor coached us in various popular dances, then arranged us in two circles, boys on the outside, girls on the inside. The music started, the circles moved in opposite directions, and, when the music stopped, your partner was the person facing you. I paid close attention to instructions and demonstrations, but I moved stiffly and couldn't take my eyes off my feet. "Bend your knees," said the instructor, and I reacted with such speed and vigor that I bumped knees with my partner. I shuffled through the box-step, the two-step, the waltz and the fox-trot, awkward and left-footed, trying to not step on my partner's feet or get too close. Some of the boys did well and some seemed to enjoy themselves, though none of us appeared to be barnyard Fred Astaires. I ended as I had begun, shuffling around the floor, watching my feet, embarrassed by my lack of savoire faire and grace, too self-conscious to be comfortable on the dance floor.

The annual fair, held in July at the fairgrounds in Janesville, was the focus of 4-H activities. Kids all over Rock County raised cows, pigs, and sheep, grooming and training them for exhibition and judging in the big arena. Those kids lived at the fairgrounds during the fair, sleeping on bales of hay above their animal's stall, spending the day bathing, currying, combing and cajoling the animal until the time came to enter the arena and compete for a blue ribbon. By the time the fair was over, the animals were probably cleaner and smelled better than their owners. The 4-H winner of the blue ribbon went home, proud of his or her work and achievement. The winning animal, however, was often sold to the highest bidder and went straight to the slaughter-house.

I didn't have the patience or desire to work with big animals. Teaching a pig to walk a straight line or a cow to stand just-so in the judging ring did not interest me. I did not want to spend my days at the fair pampering a pig or coddling a cow. Rabbits and chickens were more my style. They were small and easily managed, and required minimal care and no training. Once my rabbits and chickens were in their assigned pens at the fairgrounds and set up with food, water and bedding, I was free explore the exhibits, try the carnival rides, and see the entertainment. Best of all, rabbits and chickens were judged in their pens on a schedule set by and known only to the judges. I did not have to be present and usually learned the result when I discovered a ribbon affixed to the door of the pen.

Every entry at the fair had a chance to win an award. The ribbons awarded the manicured, fattened, and trained animals were the largest and most impressive, but baked goods, canned produce, sewing, needle point, woodwork and other handicrafts were also judged and ranked. I won ribbons with model airplanes, school projects, and vegetables from our garden. One year I had a hard time finding presentable specimens after a blight hit our tomato plants. The ones I picked did not please Dad, so, on the way to the fair, he stopped at a vegetable stand and, over my protests, picked out two handsome tomatoes. "Yours would have looked like this if it hadn't been for the blight," Dad said. Though this rationalization came from my usually straight-shooting Dad, I didn't think it was right. More surprising to me was a realization that Dad had a competitive streak and desire to win I didn't know was there. I was a little embarrassed as I added the blue ribbon those tomatoes won to my collection.

Caring for my animals was an excuse to stay with my grandparents on Garfield Street, a few blocks from the fairgrounds. For me it was an ideal arrangement: no chores, a free pass to the fair, money for snacks, with a little left over to spend on rides and games. After a quick check on my animals, I walked around the hot, humid and dusty fairgrounds, looking over machinery and art exhibits, watching the tractor pull and the horse show, and savoring the air heavy with sweat, manure, diesel oil, frying hamburgers, popcorn, and cigarettes. I loved the change and the freedom but, when we loaded my animals, exhibits, and blue ribbons in the car and headed home on the last day of the fair, I looked forward to sleeping in my own bed, getting back to my regular routine, and breathing farm air.

When we were in seventh grade my Dillenbeck classmates joined the Boy Scouts, immersing themselves so com-

pletely in scouting that it was hard for me to join in or turn
their conversation to another subject. They were not interested in my 4-H projects and I figured the only way to get
back into the action was to become a scout myself. This was
not an easy goal because I had to convince Dad that becoming a Scout would be useful and instructive for me. Only if
he accepted that premise would he hurry through milking on
Monday evenings and take me to meetings in town. With
Mom's help my plea worked and I became the first farm
boy to join the scout troop at St. Mary's school.

Breaking into a group of boys who shared the cama-
raderie of scouting and the classrooms of the parochial
school was not easy. I was an outsider, unsure how to act
and react. My cousin Dick, who lived in town and went to
St. Mary's school, was there to introduce and vouch for me
but I was viewed with bemusement and subjected to farmer
jokes. As we shook hands, one kid held up my callused hand
and compared it to his own soft palms. For basketball games,
one team was the "shirts," the other the "skins." The first
time we chose teams for basketball, I was a "skin," and heard
amused snickers when I removed my shirt to reveal my long
underwear.

Things went so poorly I considered giving up scouting,
until the night the troop leader brought boxing gloves and
put me in a makeshift ring against a cocky redheaded kid
who was reputed to be the toughest boy at St. Mary's. As
our gloves were laced up, I hoped I wouldn't suffer too badly
— physically or psychologically. Luckily, the redhead didn't
know any more about boxing than I did. We moved awk-
wardly, swung wildly and landed glancing blows, until I surprised both of us by catching him squarely in the rib cage
with my right hand, sending him to the floor. He got up

quickly, but I could see he was uncertain and cautious. After a few more wild swings I put him down again with a right to the head. As he slowly got up the scoutmaster stopped the fight, saying there were others who wanted to use the gloves. I felt the atmosphere change as I shook hands with my opponent. I heard no more remarks about long johns, hard hands, or dumb farmers.

Joining the Boy Scouts was not my first exposure to my cousin, Dick's, city life. Dick and I had begun exchanging summer visits when we were eight or nine years old. I thought a week with no chores, an ice cream parlor a block away, movie theaters within walking distance, and boys our age right next door was the perfect life. It wasn't. We rarely had money to spend on ice cream or a movie and we spent a good part of each day standing around wondering what to do. When we ran out of options someone suggested we go to the "Gully." From Dick's description of the fun he and his friends had at the Gully, I expected a combination amusement park and obstacle course. It turned out to be a grassless depression with a couple of trees and shrubs so scraggly you couldn't even hide behind one. It was just a place to hang out, a big disappointment when compared to my woods at home.

Dick had friends in the neighborhood who provided company and companionship, but there wasn't much to do. The city kids weren't lonely, they were bored. I had forty acres of woods, a secret hiding place in every building, a dog for company, and pony to ride. Friends to share these things with me would have been nice, but I was rarely bored, even when I was alone.

When friends did come to visit, I also had a swimming hole of sorts to share. During summer vacation my

Dillenbeck classmates sometimes rode their bikes out for a day of soldiering in our woods, waging war with toy guns or imaginary bows and arrows. At the end of the afternoon we'd take a swim in our pond by the woods, though sometimes we had to wait for the cows to drink and relieve themselves before we stacked our clothes on the bank and waded in, ankle deep in slimy mud. The water reached only to our knees, but we pretended to swim, our bellies sliding over mounds of mud, careful to keep our heads out of the murky water. After a swim, we sat on the grass till the sun dried us off, then dressed and headed home, everyone promising not to let Mom know that we had again ignored her frequent warning, "Don't swim in that dirty pond. It will make you sick." Surprisingly, no one seemed to suffer from dips in our murky water. Maybe over time the noxious mixture of offal, decaying vegetation, and microbes that thrived there bestowed on us an immunity to garden variety illnesses and kept us healthy.

Chapter 8

The Fannings—
My Irish Side

The first of five Fanning brothers to come to Wisconsin from County Roscommon, Ireland, was Steve, who arrived in 1869. He had been a teacher in Ireland but took jobs as a day laborer for farmers when he arrived in Rock County. He saved his money and, one by one, sent for his brothers in Ireland. Bartley came in 1872, James and John in 1875, and Michael in 1876. They all shared a small house in a woods near Lima Center, where they cut trees and sold the wood in Janesville for $5 a cord, making enough to each buy a farm near Johnstown before the arrival of the twentieth century. As might be expected, they bought farms near enough to each other to share the work of planting and harvesting, and every Sunday they went together to Mass at St. Patrick's church in Whitewater. Each Fanning brother returned home to marry an Irish girl. These unions produced a total of 43 children: eight to Steve, eleven to Michael, eight to John (including my grandfather, John James, born in 1878), and ten to Bartley. James brought up the rear with only six.

My great grandfather, John Fanning, and his wife, Elizabeth, had five girls and three boys. John James (JJ, my grandfather) was the first boy and, according to tradition, took over the 110-acre farm near Johnstown when he married in 1903. He bought the farm from his parents in 1908 for $10,000 - John and Elizabeth signed the deed of sale with "their mark," an X. JJ and Anne Manogue were married a little more than a year when their first child, Bill, was born. Their second child, Helen, my mother, was born in 1907. Six more children followed: Ray in 1911, Regina in 1913, Mary in 1914, John, Jr. in 1916, Dorothy in 1918, and Margaret, the last, in 1920.

I knew most of my aunts and uncles by their nicknames before I learned their given names. Bill was called Finning, and Ray answered to Bartley, maybe because he resembled his uncle from Ireland. Regina abandoned her given name and was always known as Dell. John, Jr. was tagged with Cuddy (later shortened to Cud) when, as a youngster, he couldn't stop talking about a trip to the stockyards in Cudahy, near Milwaukee. Mary was Maidie, probably a mispronunciation by her younger sisters. Helen was How to her siblings when I was young, and Dorothy was, of course, Dot. Margaret, the youngest — and sweetest? — was called Honey until she turned it to a more grown-up Honcie.

It was said that the Irish who settled in Rock County took pity on the Scotsmen who came and settled on the flat, fertile prairie land to the south. "Why, there's not a tree or bush on it," said the Irish, who wanted nature, not just farmland. Acquiring a farm with a bit of woods near Johnstown was quite in character for the Fanning boys from County Roscommon, even though the soil was a little sandy and had an abundance of rocks of all sizes.

The Fanning farm was about four miles from Johnstown Center, five from Lima Center and eight or nine from Milton, but the rugged dirt roads made travel treacherous and time-consuming. Uncle Bill told me of trying to take a load of 30 pigs to Lima Center in 1925: "We loaded those pigs into three wagons and did fine until we came to a mud hole so deep and wide we had to unhitch the teams and put 4 horses on each wagon to pull through that mud." It took them most of the day to make the five-mile trek.

JJ's farm had no electricity until the late 1930's, when the Rural Electrification Agency (REA) finally ran power lines past Johnstown. Until then the barn was lighted with lanterns, the cows were milked by hand and the house was powered by wet-cell batteries that lined one wall of the dirt-floored basement. The batteries were charged by a noisy generator that was cranked into action each day. The generator and batteries were disposed of when electricity was installed but a supply of candles, lamps and lanterns was kept on hand to cope with power outages that were common during the early years of REA.

In 1927, after she graduated from high school and was working in Janesville, Mom bought a Kodak box camera and began taking pictures of her family. They were usually posed in front of the weather-beaten, two-story farm house. Down spouts running from the eaves across the clapboards and into the cistern next to the warped cellar door provided the backdrop. The yard was barren. There was not a blade of grass or a shrub, though there was a fine lawn with large oaks in front of the house by the road.

Photos taken a few years later in the same place show marked improvement — a white picket fence and a glassed-in porch built over what had been a bare concrete slab at the kitchen door. People wondered, "How did JJ and Annie Fanning raise eight kids on that 110-acre farm?" It took sacrifice, ingenuity and a willingness to make do with what was at hand. Mom remembered her first mattresses of straw and feathers, windows kept closed during the heat of the summer because there were no screens, straw piled around the foundation of the house for insulation in winter, and threadbare rugs carried outside each spring, beaten with sticks, then nailed to the floor again to keep them in place. Ashes from the cook stove were removed every morning and spread on icy patches by the barn to give traction to the horses. The pump at the windmill froze solid every night in winter and the tea kettle was heated on the stove each morning to thaw it out. On the coldest days, the dipper was frozen in the water bucket in the kitchen in the morning. During one particularly cold period, their old donkey burrowed into the straw stack for warmth and wasn't found for a week. Storms brought snow so heavy it covered the fences and obliterated the road. The trip by bob sleigh to church in Milton took an hour and a half, made bearable with a stack of wool and cow skin blankets and bricks heated in the oven, wrapped in burlap and placed by the passengers' feet.

Dresses were stitched from feed sacks and high button shoes were passed from girl to girl until they wore out. The girls inherited their brothers' shoes, and sometimes even their underwear. Each summer, visiting relatives from Chicago bought pencils and tablets at Pratt's general store in Johnstown, and left them for the Fanning kids so they wouldn't have to go to school empty-handed in September. Christmas presents were few, often as simple as a new pair of stockings, an apple, an orange, or a pencil. It was a life of basic pleasures, but Mom and her sisters had few complaints about their lot, at least not when looking back after a half-century.

Grandma and Grandpa Fanning in front of their
farm house in Johnstown - 1929

Though the farm was isolated by distance and bad roads, there was social activity for the Fanning kids. This usually involved walking across the field to play with the eight Schmaling children or up the road to see what the six Malone kids were up to. In winter neighbors got together to sled down the hill not far from the Fanning farm; in summer a ball game on Sunday down at Bevans school included everyone — young and old, boys and girls. There were pheasants, ducks, and squirrels in the nearby woods and fields and Bill and Ray were avid hunters. One day they brought in twenty rabbits and turned them over to Mary and Dell to skin and clean. In summer, the family went by buggy to weekly dances at the Johnstown town hall — lively affairs with jigs and waltzes played on a fiddle and accordion.

Fanning family - about 1930. Front row - John, Jr., Margaret, Dorothy, Mary. Back row - Grandpa, Ray, Grandma, Dell, Helen, Bill

There was no shortage of food in the Fanning house. A pig and a steer were butchered in the fall and the meat hung in the stone shed next to the house all winter. As Grandma planned a meal she sent one of the kids out to cut off a piece from one of the carcasses. Every part of the animal was used: meat carved from the head and feet was cut into small pieces and compressed into head cheese; the intestines were washed and filled with sausage made from blood; and the hair was left on the hides, making blankets to use on sleigh rides in winter. The slabs of meat in the stone shed kept well during the frigid Wisconsin winter, but when the temperature began to rise in the spring the family gorged on meat, trying to finish it off before it began to spoil.

Cooking for a houseful of kids and crews of threshers in summer kept Grandma at the stove all day — preparing meals, baking bread, making pies and cakes, and canning fruits and vegetables during the summer. Grandpa, and most farmers, enjoyed a full meal three times each day: bacon and eggs for breakfast, meat and potatoes for lunch and dinner. He loved beefsteak but refused any kind of gravy, preferring to apply large dollops of butter on his potatoes, vegetables, bread, and even on his pie. When the butter supply got low he would put one of the girls in the buggy and send her off to Lima Center to buy a pound or two. It was rare that they had the money to buy more than two pounds at one time.

I was five or six when I first stayed overnight with Grandma and Grandpa. The house was full of interesting spaces for a child, like the long pantry off the kitchen with floor-to-ceiling shelves loaded with canned goods and a sliding panel for passing food into the dining room, or the storeroom upstairs filled with old chairs, quilting frames, curtain stretchers, chamber pots, lamps and lanterns. I made a game of sneaking through the house to try to surprise Grandma, starting in the kitchen, where Grandma was usually working by the stove, making my way through the dining room, and then into the living room. From there I would go through a back bedroom, which had a dark closet that led into the sewing room. The sewing room had a separate entrance into the kitchen and I would pop through to surprise Grandma (or so I thought).

Outside I explored the barn and machine shed, careful to stay away from the flock of geese that had the run of the yard. If I got too close, the old gander came after me, wings flapping, neck outstretched, beak open, pecking at my bottom as I ran screaming to the house. After my first encounter with the aggressive gander, I was careful to make a thorough survey of the yard from the kitchen window before venturing out.

In the afternoon I watched the road, waiting for Grandpa to appear on his road grader. When Bill and Ray took on the brunt of the farm work, Grandpa took a job with the county grading the gravel roads. When I saw him coming home in the evening, I ran down the road so I could get the longest ride possible. He stopped, reached down to pull me up over the big blade, and put me on his lap so I could hold the steering wheel until we turned into the yard.

When he wasn't out on the grader, Grandpa did odd jobs around the farm. One day he said, "Come on, Bobby. Let's blast some of those big rocks." I wasn't sure what blasting rocks meant, but it sounded like fun. I watched as he put several sticks of dynamite and a roll of fuse in a pail, then followed him out to a big, half-exposed boulder in the middle of a field. He dug under the boulder, laid in a couple of sticks of dynamite, and attached the fuse. He struck a match, held the flame to the fuse until it started to sputter, then said, "Now, let's run!" At a safe distance I heard a muffled blast and saw a spray of dirt. We walked back and saw the rock was split in two pieces, both small enough to be rolled onto a flat stone boat and pulled to the woods by the team of horses.

I remember Grandpa Fanning as a big, jovial man with a gift of Irish gab and a quirky sense of humor. He would come in from the field and say to his wife, Annie, "Hello, Florence, you damned fool, what kind of a day did you have today?" And they would laugh together. Grandpa liked to tease, and often told me I was full of baloney. "Yes," he would say, "I talked with your mother on the telephone last night and she told me you are just full of baloney." "Well," I said one day, fed up with the repeated accusation, "You're full of something else, too." From behind me, one of my aunts said sternly, "We don't talk that way around here." I knew I couldn't talk like that at home, either, and I turned red with embarrassment. Grandpa died soon after this episode and for many years I felt guilty for talking back to him that way. But now, sixty-some years later and with grandsons of my own, I think he probably smiled to get such sass from his first grandson.

Grandpa bought a new car in 1940, one of the first with the gear shift on the steering wheel, rather than on the floor. The first time he drove it to church in Milton he discovered he had driven all the way home in second gear. More used to the deliberate speed of a team of horses or the road grader, he never went over 30 miles an hour, which was not a strain on second gear.

Grandpa ran a strict household and the rules of the house extended to visiting grandsons. The first rule I learned was: "Don't sit in Grandpa's rocking chair." I already knew whose chair it was — it was the only one in the house with a spittoon next to it. Though Grandpa was a teetotaler and nonsmoker, he chewed tobacco, and the spittoon was often used in the evening as he sat and read. The daily job of emptying and cleaning it fell to Mary and Dell. Mary also remembers that she and Dell carried wood for the furnace in winter, cleaned the globes of the kerosene lamps when they were black with carbon from the wicks, and they were assigned to stand in a wagon by the threshing machine every summer, filling bags with oats as it came from the machine.

Grandpa's parents had signed the deed to the farm with their X, and Grandpa's education probably went no further than eighth grade. The oldest of his children went to Bevans School, a low stone structure built in 1898. According to a history of Johnstown, stone for the school came from the Newton quarry (on the farm next to the Fannings) and, when the building was razed in 1929, "the stone was used for roads by road patrolman JJ Fanning." A wooden school was built on the same site. JJ must have gone to the old stone school, though if he did I suspect the lessons were basic and the teacher minimally trained. Mary and Dell complained that they learned little from the two teachers they had at the new school. Mary said one was "dumb" and only interested in sports, and the other was smart enough but short on teaching skills. Neither the old stone school nor the new one had a well, so every morning a student was sent to fill the water bucket from the pump at a neighboring farm, and in winter a student was assigned to go to the school Sunday evening or early Monday to start a fire in the stove so the room would be warm when the teacher arrived.

Whatever his own schooling, JJ valued education and insisted that at least one of his girls become a teacher. Bill quit school after fourth grade and Ray after two years of high school. Mom was the first to go on to high school, graduating in 1927, but she was not interested in more education or in becoming a teacher. Instead, she went to Janesville to work in department stores and as a telephone operator until she married. Dell and Mary finished eight years at Bevans school but neither passed the high school qualifying test. Dell was not interested in more schooling, but Mary rode a horse each day to remedial classes in

Johnstown, passed the test and entered high school at the end of the summer. After graduating from high school, Mary took the entrance test required of prospective teachers, but missed a crucial question and did not qualify. It was up to Dorothy and Honcie to provide JJ with a teacher. Both earned teaching certificates from Whitewater Normal College and JJ had two teachers in the family shortly before he died, suddenly, of a heart attack, on November 5, 1942.

Grandpa had complained of a burning in his chest, but he appeared to be in good health and the family doctor said his heart sounded fine. But a diet of beefsteak, butter and chocolate candy can create problems, even for an active farmer. Clogged arteries were difficult to detect at that time and heart surgery was far in the future. There was no treatment for heart trouble at that time, even if the problem had been detected.

Grandma was devastated at his sudden death. Her beloved husband, still young, seemingly healthy, was gone in an instant. As was the tradition, the casket was displayed in the back bedroom and a steady stream of mourners came to offer condolences, to reminisce, and to console the widow. Mom said Grandma fell into a depression so deep she was hospitalized for a time. But, she was tough and resilient and gradually recovered her spirits. Ray was still at home, running the farm. Dell left her job in town and returned to help. The three lived on the farm until Dell married Ward Cullen in 1945, and began farming, not far away. When Ray married a year later, Grandma came to visit us. She spent a few weeks with us, then went to Dell's for a few more weeks, and then to Mary's. Until she passed away peacefully in 1958, Grandma continued to spend extended visits with her daughters. There didn't seem to be a formula or calendar that determined where she would go or how long she would stay; she just seemed to show up. One day I would come home from school and she would be in our kitchen helping Mom fix a meal or sitting in the rocking chair in the living room, knitting.

Our family and every family welcomed her visits, and she never complained about her transient life. In fact, she didn't complain about anything, and could always be found with a smile and a good word for everyone. Dad enjoyed her company and our home seemed a little warmer when she was with us. Ward didn't seem to want her to leave. Wherever she was staying, Ward would stop by and plead, "Grandma, when are you coming back? I am starving at home." (Which was a lie, of course. Dell was a great cook and Ward never wanted for a good meal.)

My early memories of Grandma are of her in her own kitchen, wearing a house dress and stained flowered apron, cooking over the cast-iron stove. In the snapshots Mom took in front of their house she wears a house dress and apron; these were her working clothes. We also have pictures of her dressed for church and special occasions — stylish in high shoes, dark dress, black coat and simple hat. Her wardrobe was limited — she traveled from house to house with a single suitcase — but she was always neatly and fashionably dressed.

When she was with us, Grandma helped Mom with the cooking, but as she grew older she spent most of her time patching our clothes, darning our socks, and knitting. Her knitting was basic and simple; her specialty was mittens. In fact, I never saw her knit anything but mittens, which she made in two sizes — large for boys, small for girls — all exactly the same but for color. Her mittens were distinctive because the end of the thumb and the top of the mitten always came to a point, not like the rounded machine-made mittens we got in stores. We loved Grandma's tightly knit, pointed mittens because they were unique — and very warm.

Helen Fanning and Al Knopes at the Fanning farm - about 1929

She taught us card games like Hearts and Old Maid, showed us how to make a cat's cradle with a piece of string, and challenged us to games of checkers. Of course, when we played games with Grandma, we always won. But we noted that when she sat down for a game of cards with adults she played to win.

Grandma was easy-going and didn't show concern or disapproval over the antics of her grandchildren. Mom was not happy when my good green sweater was ripped off my back in a St. Patrick's Day brawl at my high school, but

Grandma was delighted that I felt Irish enough to wear a green sweater and defend the name of Ireland. She went immediately for her sewing kit and repaired the sweater so I could wear it again the next day. When she heard I had gone skinny-dipping in a nearby pond while some girls were nearby, she said, "If they see something they haven't seen before, let them throw their hat at it." I never figured out what that saying meant, but I liked her attitude.

A studio photo shows her as a young lady - eighteen or nineteen, bright-eyed, her hair cut short with a curly fringe over her forehead, a pendant on a black choker around her neck and a collared dress with fluffs at the shoulders. She has a serious expression and looks straight ahead as though looking into her future, but her eyes seem to twinkle. She must have been a lively participant in jigs and reels at parties when she was a girl and at dances at the Johnstown Town Hall with JJ. She was still dancing in her eighties; we have a photo of her and Uncle Bill on the dance floor in 1955.

In an informal picture taken in the late 1920's, she and JJ stand in front of their house. She is wearing a house dress and high button shoes, her hair is piled loosely on her head, and she is smiling the little smile she always had. She has a grandmotherly appearance, though her first grandchild (me) is still several years in the future. She looks happy and content, but I think the photo shows some of the strain of delivering eight children in sixteen years, and raising them in a house without running water, electricity, or a toilet. Despite being pregnant often and always having an infant by her side, she cooked, baked, washed and mended clothes for her growing family, and fed gangs of threshers and silo fillers.

Grandma was gentle and kind, but above all she was

tough. She supported JJ on the farm, raised a large family, and took care of her own needs. When her teeth were bothering her, she went by buggy to consult a dentist in Janesville. The dentist recommended false teeth as the only solution. She agreed, he pulled all her teeth, and she got back in the buggy and drove home, a ten-mile, two-hour ride over rutted gravel roads. It must have been an excruciating trip.

She died at our house on November 5, 1958, sixteen years to the day after her husband. She got up in the night, said to my mother, who slept on a cot nearby, "I'm all right, Helen," went back to bed and suffered a fatal heart attack.

Chapter 9

The Knopes—
My German Side

My grandparents on the Knopes side were German-speaking immigrants who came to the United States separately and met in Janesville.

My grandfather, Henry Knopes, was born in Luxembourg to Joseph Knopes and his wife, Anna, in 1868. Joseph was a carpenter, but probably knew something about farming, since Luxembourg is an agricultural country. Joseph and Anna had nine children, the first four were girls, followed by five boys. Susan was born in 1856 but lived only two years; Elizabeth came in 1859, Marie in 1860, and Margaret in 1861. The first boy, Mathias, was born in 1863, then came Harry, in 1866, followed by Henry, my grandfather, in 1868, Dominic in 1871, and Nicolas in 1874. Mathias died at age eight.

Elizabeth and Marie married and stayed in Luxembourg. The boys, and later, Margaret, emigrated to the United States, having heard that in America money was plentiful and easy to get. Harry and Henry might have come to America together about 1888, when Harry was 22, and Henry 20. Whether they traveled together or not, Harry and Henry both went west and found work on a sheep ranch. Harry lived in Idaho for several years before moving on to Washington to establish his own sheep ranch. His granddaughter said that at one time his herd was the largest in the state. Nicolas came to America in 1890, when he was only 16, first settling in Minnesota, then moving to Colton, Washington, in 1900. Nicolas' grandson believes that Harry, Margaret and Nicolas all moved to Washington state about the same time.

Life in the west and sheep herding did not hold my grandfather Henry's interest, and after one year he moved east to Janesville, Wisconsin. Why did he choose Wisconsin? Maybe he had a contact in the large German community there, or he might have met someone on the passage over who was going to Janesville. Whatever the reason, southern Wisconsin, with its fertile land and rolling hills, must have reminded him of Luxembourg. Henry found work as a hired man on a farm, receiving room and board and a small weekly wage. He soon met Mary Manthey, a girl in her twenties, who had recently arrived from Milgast, Germany, and was working as a housekeeper. Though she was already engaged when Henry arrived on the scene, he won her over and they were married in 1900. In 1901, they bought an 80-acre farm in Afton Township, south of Janesville, and started a family.

Dominic came to Janesville and established a tailor shop at 16 Main Street. His obituary in 1934 stated, "Dominic had worked as a tailor in Janesville for the past 35 years," so he must have reached Janesville in the mid-1890s, perhaps on Henry's recommendation. "He was a very good tailor," Dad said, "making fine suits for bankers and businessmen." Dominic had a severe limp because of a boyhood accident, a handicap that might have kept him from going into farming as his brothers had. He never married, and over the years he made his home in various boarding hotels in Janesville.

Grandma and Grandpa Knopes wedding portrait - 1900

Les, Alfred and Anna Knopes - about 1908.

Henry and Mary's first child, Anna, was born in 1901, followed by a son, Leslie, in 1902. My father, Alfred, was born in 1904. The last two children were Harry, 1909, and

Edna, 1911. By 1916, the family had outgrown the 80-acre farm, so Henry sold it for $9,000 and bought 160 acres north of Janesville — for $100 an acre. The mortgage of $14,200 Henry took out to buy the property was paid off in ten years.

The family packed their possessions in the farm wagon for the move and put the boys in charge of the dairy herd for the 15-mile trek. Dad said it was a boring walk until they got to Janesville's residential neighborhoods, where they wore themselves out running and yelling to keep the cows from feasting on gardens and lawns.

The farm my grandparents bought on Humes Road was platted and sold by the federal government in 1848, the year Wisconsin became a state. A handwritten abstract shows Henry Knopes to be the fifth owner of the property. The buildings were in good condition, the black soil was more than a foot deep and the 40-acres of woods with a small pond were ideal for pasturing a dairy herd. An orchard next to the house (maybe planted by Henry and his family) provided apples, cherries and pears. A row of grape vines flourished behind the garage, providing enough grapes each fall to make a winter's supply of jam and jelly, and even a couple kegs of wine.

Though German was their first language, the Knopes' kids quickly learned English when they enrolled at the nearby school. Dad quit school after eighth grade to work full-time on the farm, while his brothers preferred careers in town. Les worked at the Corona Pen Factory in Milton before becoming an electrician with the Wisconsin Power and Light Company. Harry entered the business world early, becoming joint owner of the Knopes and Peck feed mill in Janesville when he was just 18. Harry left the feed mill in the early

1930's to drive for the W.R. Arthur Company, transporting new cars from the Chevrolet plant in Janesville to dealers. Grandpa Knopes, after he turned the farm over to my Dad and moved to town, did office work in the feed mill. Edna was a secretary at the Parker Pen Company until she married.

Anna did not live to see how her siblings developed. She was still in high school when she contracted tuberculosis, a disease which was little understood at the time. The prescribed treatment was fresh air, and the screened porch that overlooked the lawn and road became Anna's bedroom. There she endured the heat and humidity of Wisconsin summers and the freezing temperatures of winter. Some survived this therapy and lived long lives, but Anna's condition did not improve. She died just before her twentieth birthday in 1919, and is buried in Mt. Olivet Cemetery in Janesville, with her parents.

By the turn of the century Dominic's tailoring business was well-established and he routinely rode the Interurban train, which ran between Janesville and Beloit, out to the Afton farm on weekends. After Mom and Dad were married in 1930, Dominic was a frequent visitor to our farm. Mom said he was a "nice old guy," the kindest words she had to say about any of her in-laws.

Over the years Dominic invested his earnings from his tailor shop in Wisconsin Power and Light stocks, accumulating a portfolio of $20,000. He expected this safe, local utility to finance his retirement, but the stock market crash in 1929 made his certificates all but worthless. Dominic and the nation sank into a deep depression. Though his shop was still listed in the 1931 Janesville Business Directory, he continued working until 1932. "He spent his last years looking in his wallet and shaking his head," Dad said.

Dominic (seated) and Nicolas Knopes

Unable to take care of himself in his last months, Dominic moved to a county-run facility for the aged and ill, perhaps to a ward for the indigent. Some thought that Grandpa and Grandma Knopes should have taken him in, but by then he was probably emotionally unstable and too sick for home care. He died November 10, 1934, at age 63, and was buried in the family plot in Mt. Olivet next to his niece, Anna. Grandpa Knopes inherited the Power and Light stock and sold it for $1,100.

Farming had already begun to change when Grandpa bought the farm on Humes road. Power lines brought electricity to light our farm buildings, power a milking machine and pump our water. Around 1920, Dad convinced Grandpa to buy a tractor. "He couldn't believe how much land that tractor could plow in a day," Dad said. About the same time, the county improved our road from dirt to gravel and Grandpa bought a Model A Ford. In the evening, after milking, Dad often took the car into town to shoot pool and have a drink or two at one of the taverns. On weekends, he drove to dances, band concerts and ice cream socials in the area. Sometimes he covered more than 100 miles, going from farm to farm over treacherous country roads, gathering a load of partygoers as he went.

At a band concert in the park in Milton, Dad met Helen Fanning and began a courtship that led to their marriage. Mom had grown up on the hardscrabble Fanning farm in Johnstown and was independent minded. She was the first of the family to go to high school, driving a donkey cart to Milton when the weather was good and boarding with relatives in town during the harsh winters. She never complained about the daily two-hour trip in the donkey cart, but she was unhappy about having to miss lunch hour activities with her classmates because "I had to go to the stable across the street to feed that stupid donkey." She graduated from high school in 1927, and immediately looked for work in Janesville. She was a clerk in Wunderlich's department store for a while, then became a telephone operator. Her last job before marriage was at the Parker Pen Company. She lived in town during the week, sharing a room with a friend, and returned to the Fanning farm on weekends. With one of her first paychecks, she bought a Kodak box camera and began a photo album. The first few pages of the album contain shots of Fanning family members in front of the farmhouse, but photos soon appeared of Al Knopes, nattily dressed in suit and bow tie, "The Boyfriend" written on the margin of each photo. There were other suitors (her sisters said "many, many"), but she and Al were married on November 30, 1930, at St. Mary's church in Milton Junction.

After a honeymoon in Michigan, they set up house-keeping on the Knopes' farm. Dad would run the farm and share expenses and income, half and half, with his parents, who would move to town. "Don't move in there until the Knopeses move out," Mom's parents cautioned. That was their way of hinting that her new father- and mother-in-law might be looking to share housing as well as income from the farm. If there was a discussion or negotiation on such an idea, it was short. Grandpa and Grandma Knopes purchased a house on Garfield Street in Janesville and Mom and Dad took over the farm and farmhouse.

Though they must have been pleased that their son and his bride would continue to develop the farm, it must have also been difficult for Henry, 62, and Mary, only 56, both healthy and strong, to suddenly exchange a thriving farm, where every day was filled with hard work and challenge, for a small house with a tiny yard on a quiet street in Janesville.

It was well known that Mary preferred work in the field to housekeeping. She was reputed to have been out shock-ing oats until a few hours before Dad was born, and back working in the garden the day after. Settled in town, there was only housework to keep her busy, so the house was always immaculate. In the tidy garden out back, tended by both Henry and Mary, no weed survived more than a few hours after showing its head.

There was just not enough to keep them occupied those first years in town, so Henry and Mary regularly drove the Model A back to the farm to help. Grandma helped with noon meals for threshers and silo fillers, while Grandpa drove the team of horses on the wagon. Even though she could use the help, Mom was not pleased to share her kitchen with her mother-in-law or to listen to her advice on cooking, children or caring for chickens. It was a clash of cultures and of strong-willed personalities. Despite the tension, however, there was never a blowup or altercation and Mary's visits gradually tapered off as she involved herself in card groups and church work with German-speaking friends and relatives. She approached card games the same way she approached work: with intensity and determination. After Mary played a losing hand, her sister-in-law, Agatha Manthey, who was her regular partner, occasionally reminded her, "Mary, relax, you can't win every time."

Henry was a farmer who had no interest in card playing or church work. He continued to come to the farm several days a week, walking the three miles from his house after he sold the Model A. In his seventies he developed arthritis and walked with a pronounced limp, but that didn't stop him from visiting us. He always walked directly to the granary where he kept his work clothes hanging on a nail inside the sliding door, changed, then went looking for Dad to see what help was needed. Dad usually harnessed the team of horses and sent Grandpa out to cut and rake hay or cultivate tobacco. Sitting firmly upright on the steel seat, Grandpa looked serene and content. He was where he belonged, on the farm, holding the reins, guiding the horses around the field.

Grandpa Knopes

Dad appreciated Grandpa's help but Mom saw his daily presence as free loading and was constantly, if quietly, critical. She called him "The Old Fossil" (though not when anyone was around to hear) and complained when he stayed for the evening meal. "Why should we have to feed him? He's already getting half of what we make!" she complained. It was an unfair criticism. He ate little, came into the house only at mealtime, and was helpful to Dad. But, since he was often at our house, he became the focus of Mom's disaffection with her in-laws. She resented what they took and how little they gave in return. "It wasn't fair," she insisted, "that they came out any time they wanted, took a pint of cream and gallon of milk right out of the milk cans, and when we butchered in the fall, they got half the pig or beef to share."

It wasn't the amount they took that bothered Mom: it was their sense of entitlement and the lack of gratitude. If any of them had come out to help at harvest time, Mom's discontent and resentment might have been moderated. "It's too bad Al can't be here tonight," one in-law remarked to Mom at the wake for Edna's husband. "It's too bad he never gets any help with chores so he would be able to get away," she retorted in a rare and uncharacteristic outburst from someone who religiously avoided confrontation. Mom was the sort who usually bit her tongue and remained silent.

Despite this underlying tension, we had regular contact with the Knopes family. Dad took his grist to Harry's feed mill in Janesville and we often stopped at Garfield Street on our way to or from town. We got together there every Christmas eve to exchange presents and sometimes for Thanksgiving dinner. At these events, we cousins entertained ourselves with games upstairs or in the basement while the men drank beer and the women had tea or coffee in the living room. Compared to the extravagant buffet meals, noisy card games and boisterous banter at a gathering of Fannings, these were subdued affairs, annual rituals that brought us together for only a few hours.

In summer, during the 4-H fair, I stayed with Grandpa and Grandma Knopes. The fairgrounds was only a few blocks away from their house on Garfield Street so I could walk over to care for my animals. When I was in high school, if a blizzard was forecast, I stayed at Garfield Street so I would not miss classes if our road was closed by snow. I remember soaking in the big bathtub, paging through the books written in old German, and the neat, clean, silent rooms.

But it was not a house of warmth or communication. I cannot recall a single conversation with either Grandma or Grandpa. In the evening we sat in silence in the living room, reading. In the morning Grandma asked what I wanted for breakfast, prepared it, and watched while I ate. I think we were at a loss on how to react to each other. Grandma was direct, plain spoken and given to curt pronouncements in her heavy German accent. "Vell," she would say, "Dat is not de vay ve should do it." She did not engage in small talk or show much interest in the activities of her grandchildren. If she ever laughed or smiled, I missed it. Wondering if the lack of communication had been my fault, I checked to see if Shirl and my cousins had a different relationship with our German grandparents. Their recollections were the same.

The longest conversation I remember having with Grandma came when the blizzard I was in town to avoid closed down the city, including all schools. With nothing else to do in the morning I shoveled out the walk and driveway. Seeing this, the next door neighbor asked if I would do hers as well. When I finished she asked how much I charged. I had no idea how much the job was worth and said, "Whatever you think is right." "No, no. How much do you want?" she insisted. After several exchanges in this vein and anxious to get away, I mumbled, "Three dollars." She gave me the money, went in her house and immediately called Grandma to complain about my greed. Grandma did not ask me why I had demanded such a lofty fee, she only glared at me and said I had better go right out and shovel the neighbor's driveway, too. I wanted to explain that I would have taken whatever her neighbor wanted to give me, but she was not interested. Her look implied that I had taken advantage of her innocent neighbor.

Knopes family l-r Edna, Les, Grandma, Harry, Alfred

I saw Grandpa as the opposite of Grandma — quiet, gentle, and reserved, but with a twinkle in his eye and a tentative smile always at the corner of his mouth. His wife did the talking when they were together, but with Dad and other men, he was chatty and outgoing. His hearing was poor, he had arthritis, liver spots covered the back of his hands and fading pigmentation left white patches on his cheeks. He seemed to me to be much older than Grandma, who did not appear to age. Grandpa was so self-effacing and easygoing I wondered why Mom was so hard on him. I suspect he had the same outlook and personality as his brother Dominic, and, if Mom had known him under other circumstances, she would probably have pronounced him, too, "a nice old guy."

In the long run, he was more than a nice guy. He showed conviction and courage when, in 1948, 80-years old, diagnosed with liver cancer and ready to wrap up his affairs, he told Dad he would sell him the farm for $16,000, the price he had paid in 1916. Although she signed the deed, Grandma did not agree with the terms of the sale and made Grandpa sleep in the basement for several weeks afterwards. Grandpa died at home in September, 1948, bloated and jaundiced from the liver cancer.

When Grandma died five years later, in 1953, we found out how deep had been her opposition to the sale. According to the terms of her will, her estate was divided equally among Leslie, Harry and Edna. Alfred received only $100, because "he had been provided for during my life." It was a surprising and vindictive bequest that left Dad angry and bitter. Whether he blamed his siblings for influencing the will or for lack of regard over the injustice, in a stormy meeting he broke off contact with them. It was several years before he and his brothers came together again. His estrangement from Edna lasted until 1980, when she — who had been bridesmaid at Mom and Dad's wedding — was invited to their fiftieth wedding anniversary celebration.

I can only wonder how Grandpa decided on the price when he sold Dad the farm. In 1948, it was certainly worth more than $100 an acre. That may have been Grandma's objection. I suppose Dad's willingness to take over the farm, to work it on halves, and to make it a success were factors in Grandpa's decision. He and Dad shared a love of farming and Dad's success had enabled Henry and Mary to live well in town. Grandpa's regular visits to the farm — the opportunities to get back on the land, drive the horses, and do useful work — were probably factors, too. They worked together for many years and a close bond developed between them. After Grandpa's funeral Dad lingered at the grave site, and we saw him wipe his eyes and blow his nose. "They were very close," someone behind me remarked. Those were the only tears I ever saw Dad shed.

Chapter 10

The Family
That Works Together . . .

Though Dad's work was mostly outside and Mom's was in the house, in the spring and summer many jobs overlapped and became family activities.

In March, for example, we all went to the hatchery in town and loaded 300 baby chicks — six boxes, 50 to a box — into our car. Back home, we carried the boxes to the brooder house, already heated to 80 degrees, removed the chicks one by one, dipped their tiny bills in the water tray to orient them to their new home, and placed them gently on the sawdust-covered floor. Over the next month we checked on them several times each day, making sure the feed and water containers were full and there was no sign of sickness or cannibalism. (When chickens, no matter how small, see blood or weakness in the flock, they gather round and peck mercilessly until the victim dies.) By mid-April, the little yellow balls of fluff we had brought home had doubled in size, grown small white feathers, and were outside foraging in the grass for bugs. The roosters were developing combs, not knowing that this destined them for the frying pan in the fall. The females of the flock would grow to adulthood and provide us with eggs through the winter.

Dad and me

Spring was also when Dad handed us rakes and clippers and said, "It's time to clean up the yard," meaning we would spend the day raking dead grass and leaves from the lawn, trimming the shrubbery, and collecting tree branches broken off in winter storms. The debris we collected we dumped in the ditch by the road. When the cleanup was complete, Dad handed me a box of matches and let me set the pile of dry grass, dead leaves and sticks ablaze. The embers would still be glowing when I went up to bed in the evening and the fragrance of burning leaves filled the air as I drifted off to sleep.

Planting the garden was also a cooperative job. After Dad plowed a half-acre plot, we pulled strings taut between stakes to ensure straight rows, dug shallow furrows along the strings, and dropped in the seeds — leaf lettuce, cucumbers, beets, carrots, tomatoes, and string beans. The lettuce, cucumbers and tomatoes provided us with salad though the summer. The beets, string beans, carrots and peas Mom cooked for meals, and she canned those we did not eat.

We grew 15-acres of peas for the local canning company so did not plant them in our garden. For several years we had a pea viner behind our barn — a revolving cylinder that somehow removed the peas from the pods. The pea vines were brought in from the field on trucks and fed into the viner. As the peas were shaken out of the pods, they fell through screens, dropped into boxes, and were taken to the cannery. The vines were stacked for winter cattle feed. Mom took what peas she needed for cooking and canning right from the boxes at the viner. When Dad quit growing peas and moved on to other crops, neighbors who still grew peas for the canning company let us take ripe vines from their fields before the harvest. The only drawback was that we had to sit and remove the peas from the pods by hand.

In the fall Dad called us together to pick potatoes and apples. Potato vines grow above ground with the potatoes underneath. Dad turned over each plant with a fork. Shirl,

Mom and I followed with buckets, picking up the exposed potatoes and breaking up clods of dirt so as not to miss even the smallest tuber. We moved along the rows, each carrying a pail, stooping to pick up the potatoes. When my back began to tire, I tried moving on my knees, pushing the pail in front of me.

I didn't like the job and showed it by moving slower and slower, until Dad finally yelled, "Bob, let's go. Get a move on! You're way behind everyone else!" Mom and Shirl just kept on stooping and picking.

Picking apples was easier and cleaner work. As Mom and I picked the lower branches of the apple trees clean (Shirl was too short to be much help) Dad climbed the wooden ladder to get the apples beyond our reach. Once, tired of constantly moving the heavy ladder, Dad nailed a coffee can to the end of a long pole and tried to jiggle the apples into it. Only the ripest apples came loose, and some of those fell out as he lowered his contraption to the ground. He finally gave up the experiment, got back on the ladder, and finished picking. Before we carried the apples down to the cellar to be stored over the winter we inspected each one for bruising. One bad apple could spoil the whole lot, as the saying goes.

Dad liked tinkering and trying out ideas to make jobs easier or more efficient. In the winter or when it rained and he couldn't be in the field, he used his spare time to repair and build things. It took him a whole winter to overhaul the tractor engine because he wasn't sure just how to get all the pieces back together. That didn't deter him. "I can take it apart. If I can't get it back together then I'll pay a mechanic," he said. He was usually able to figure it all out and rarely had to call on a mechanic. He also made a table and chair for me when I was small and built a drop-top desk that Shirl and I used until we were in high school. And, using an discarded truck axle and old lumber, he created a light trailer that we pulled behind the car for years.

When I began hinting that I wanted a pair of skis for Christmas, Dad said, "We can make a pair of skis and you won't have to wait for Santa Claus." He filed the tips of two narrow boards to a point, soaked them in water for a several days, weighted the ends with bricks and propped them against the wall in the basement. When the wood dried, the pointed ends curved up. Bindings he made by nailing strips of harness leather to the boards. I waxed the bottoms with sealing wax, grabbed two tobacco lathes to use as ski poles, and took my new skis to the hill by the woods, planning to glide down the slope. But my skis did not glide. In fact, I could barely push them forward through the snow. It turned out that the wood we used for the skis was soft and rough, and the sealing wax I had applied just rolled off in the snow. I pushed my way down the hill with my ski poles but gave up after a few tries. My homemade skis were a disappoint-ment, but I still admired Dad's ingenuity and his readiness to try new things. That Christmas I got a pair of real skis.

Mom and Dad worked together to build our farm into a successful enterprise. Dad once said, "Helen and I did it together." This was definitely true, though Mom would liked to have had a bit more say in how money was spent. Dad was willing to make major purchases of things that were antiquated or worn out — a carpet, a stove, or a refrigerator — but the purely cosmetic changes, like remodeling, never made it to the top of his priority list. Something more impor-tant always came along to use available funds. But money from the sale of chickens and eggs was Mom's, and she began to put this aside for her own to-do list.

In the fall, she always had more orders for young roosters (called fryers because they were best fried in butter) than she could handle. When the roosters reached maturity, Dad caught them, removed their heads with a hatchet, and dipped them, one by one, in boiling water to loosen the feathers for easier removal. The birds were picked clean of feathers and laid out on an improvised table in the yard. Mom removed the innards and cut the birds into pan-sized pieces, after which they were ready for delivery. Chickens lay eggs year-round but are most productive in winter. Some winter weeks we sold more than 60 dozen eggs from our flock of about 150 hens. With a dozen eggs selling for less than 50 cents and a fryer bringing only two or three dollars, Mom's fund grew slowly, so she sometimes took on outside jobs, like cleaning house for her divorced cousin. For several months she took care of his house and laundry, but when it came time to pay, her cousin, always short of cash, asked Mom if she would accept a heifer from his herd instead of cash. "I didn't have much choice," she said. "If I waited for cash it might never come. But I knew that if we brought the cow home, it would go right into our herd. It did, and I never got a cent for all that work I did." Still, the fund grew and, by 1942, she had enough to remodel the kitchen. Twenty years later she had saved another $814.80 and bought new cabinets and a propane stove for the kitchen.

Mom did what she could to help Dad with his work, but she had a busy regular routine that included cooking our meals, making beds, cleaning the house, washing and mending our clothes, helping with homework, and getting Shirl and me, lunches in hand, on the road in time to get to school before the bell rang. Still, when she could, Mom took on jobs that freed Dad to spend more time in the field, like cleaning the milking machines each morning. In the afternoon she reassembled and carried them to the barn in the afternoon, giving Dad a few minutes to relax over dinner before going to the barn to start milking. Until I was big enough to take over the job, Mom drove the team of horses, and later the tractor, on the rope that pulled hay from the wagon into the hayloft of the barn. Driving the team of horses was a tough job because, at the end of the pull, the team had to be turned around and driven back to the starting point at the barn. One had to be careful that the team, and the driver, did not become tangled in the hay rope or in the harness as the horses turned. The tractor was easier because it could be put in reverse as the rope was being reset. Mom never let on that she hated the job, but told me later, "I was always afraid the rope would snap and kill me." At the time she didn't complain or hesitate. It was work that had to be done and she was the only one available to do it.

Sunday mornings we went as a family to Mass at St. Mary's church in Janesville, though when there were crops to be planted, we sometimes had to split up. On planting days Dad got up at 4:30 a.m., did the milking, went to 6 a.m. Mass and was home and in the field by 7:30. Shirl and I went with Mom to the 9 o'clock service. The rest of the year, Dad finished chores in time to join us at the 9 a.m. service. In winter, Shirl and I attended catechism classes, which were held after Mass in the parochial school next to the church. Though the temperature was sometimes near zero, Mom and Dad waited in the car, reading the Sunday paper and running the heater to ward off the chill while Shirl and I went to class. It was cold in the car, but not much warmer for us in the school. The school heating system was turned off after the last class on Friday, and by Sunday morning the rooms were painfully cold. We sat in the frigid classroom in our winter coats and gloves, watching our breath as we recited the prayers we had learned during the week. On the coldest days the teaching nun wore gloves and at least one wool sweater under her habit. The lessons we learned for those classes are long forgotten, but I still remember the cold.

My family

Entering St. Mary's church as a child was an awesome experience for me. It was the biggest building I had ever seen and I marveled at the vaulted ceiling that was higher than the top of our barn. I craned my neck to trace the curving lines where the supporting pillars of onyx and Italian marble melded into the huge vaults. I wondered how the windows of imported antique stained glass were made and why the marble altar rail stayed cool in summer. While the priest droned on those Sunday mornings, saying the Mass in Latin and giving sermons I rarely paid attention to, I inspected the wonders of the building — the marble altar, the lights hanging on heavy chains, and statues of saints mounted on the walls. And I toyed with the little snaps on the backs of the pews where men hung their hats until Dad slapped my hand.

I also remember hearing, in the quiet of the church, Dad's audible breathing. At home he was never without a cigarette, and, over the years, he developed a smoker's cough and labored breathing. I was sure everybody in the church could hear him. Of course, at that time most men smoked and smokers wheezed. I would have heard a similar wheezing no matter where I sat. As I listened to Dad I decided that smoking could not be good for one's health. Peer pressure and a desire to appear cool led me to try smoking in high school, but it was not as pleasurable or satisfying as advertisements promised, so it was not hard for me to quit when the idea that smoking looked "cool" had passed.

When he was working, Dad always had a burning cigarette between his lips. I watched, fascinated, as the fire moved slowly towards his mouth. When there seemed to be nothing left but the glowing tip, he took a pack of cigarettes from the upper pocket of his bib overalls and used the stub to light a fresh one. During World War II, when cigarettes were rationed, Dad rolled his own, dropping a line of tobacco from a small cloth bag onto a piece of cigarette paper, licking the pre-glued edge to seal it, and twisting the ends to keep the tobacco from falling out. To light his cigarettes he pulled a wooden kitchen match across the seat of his overalls or flicked the head with his thumb, and the match head burst into flame, throwing off sparks and the smell of sulfur. When matches in little covered books arrived in the late 1930's, these light-anywhere matches almost disappeared. Matchbooks were safer to carry and use, but I missed the pyrotechnics of the old wooden matches.

One day, without announcement, comment or outward struggle, Dad threw away an open pack of cigarettes and never bought another. I asked him later why he quit so suddenly. He said, "I shoveled a load of ground corncobs off the truck that afternoon. The dust was terrible and the wind blew it all back in my face. The next morning I couldn't even get a breath. I figured cigarettes weren't helping, so I quit."

We ate dinner at noon and supper in the evening. In summer we were together for both meals. In winter, when Shirl and I were in school, we were together as a family only for supper. Conversation at dinner was about work done in the morning and work to be done in the afternoon. The radio was on so Dad could hear the noon reports on stock prices. If the price of pork was up he might decide to take a load of pigs to the Cudahy stockyard in Milwaukee or to Jones Meats in Jefferson. If the price was down he would wait a while longer. At supper during the school year, we talked about school and projects we were working on. I sometimes described a heavy homework assignment, hoping Dad would say, "Maybe you'd better skip milking tonight and do your school work." That never happened. Once he said that if I could eat 12 pancakes for supper I wouldn't have to help with milking that evening. But after I choked down the last bite of the twelfth pancake, Dad said he was only kidding and that we had better get started on the chores. Only serious injury or illness could get me out of evening milking.

Shirlee feeding chickens

After milking and chores were done, Dad washed up and sat down to read the newspaper at the kitchen table,

while Mom ironed, darned socks or mended our clothes. Sometimes Dad sat in his reclining chair in the living room to read *The Farm Journal* or one of the pulp western magazines he enjoyed, but he soon fell asleep with the magazine on his lap. We were usually in bed by 9:00 PM.

When I had finished my chores and there were no friends to play with (which was most of the time), I read. I began with comic books — Donald Duck, Mickey Mouse — then added action heroes like Superman, Batman and Robin, Spiderman, and the Flash. When Classic Comics, cartoon depictions of well-known books like *The Man in the Iron Mask, The Three Musketeers,* and *The Last of the Mohicans,* appeared on the magazine rack at the Star Billiard, I added these to my collection. I had so many comic books that Mom made a bookcase out of an orange crate, covered it with a piece of chintz cloth and insisted I keep them all there. She was tired of finding them in every room of the house, she said.

By the time I was twelve, we had subscriptions to popular magazines, like *Life, Look, The Saturday Evening Post,* and *Colliers,* publications that carried good writing and plenty of photos. Since neither Mom nor Dad read much more than the *Janesville Daily Gazette* and farm magazines, I suppose the subscriptions were taken to broaden my horizons. They did that, and more. Photos and features in *Look* and *Life* introduced me to a world beyond Wisconsin and I was quickly hooked on the serial stories in *Colliers* and *The Saturday Evening Post.*

Magazines got me interested in books, which led me to the stationery store in Janesville that carried the latest editions on a shelf in the back. I gave up buying toys and used my allowance to start a library of books on the war, like

Thirty Seconds Over Tokyo, written by a pilot who flew with Jimmy Doolittle on the first U.S. air raid on Japan, *God is My Co-Pilot*, by an American pilot with the Flying Tigers in China, and *Tarawa*, a journalist's firsthand account of U.S. Marines taking an island in the South Pacific, which I still own.

To keep me in books Mom suggested we go to the public library in Janesville to apply for a library card. Always frugal, she was reluctant to pay the two-dollar fee for those who did not live within the city limits. Before we went in she coached me to say I lived with my grandparents, not in the country. So, when the librarian asked where I lived I replied, "Garfield Street." I was not prepared for a follow-up question. "What school do you go to?" she asked. "Dillenbeck," I answered truthfully, killing my chances of getting a library card. "Why didn't you say Adams?" Mom asked as we left. I was disappointed to go away empty-handed. We were not so poor that the fee was impossible. I think that, after being caught in our little misrepresentation, Mom was embarrassed and flustered, and only wanted to get away.

Chapter 11

Friends

My parents came from different backgrounds, but their common interest was people. They had a special talent for making folks feel welcome and they connected with everyone they met, young and old. They accepted my friends with such cordiality and sincerity that many dropped in to visit them long after I had left Wisconsin. The people who visited us over the years, the hired men who worked for Dad, the merchants we dealt with in town and our neighbors — all were an important part of my growing up.

Mom's sisters dropped in after shopping in town, friends came by on their way home from work at General Motors and Parker Pen, and regulars from the Milton Avenue taverns, tired of their drinking companions and needing a sandwich, dropped by in the evening with a six-pack of beer to tell incoherent stories. These visitors always sat in the kitchen, sooner or later accepting a cookie, a piece of pie or a sandwich. Mom couldn't stand to see anyone without some kind of food to munch on. Hoboes (itinerants) who wandered the countryside during the Depression looking for work were not turned away. Dad let them sleep in the barn overnight and Mom fixed them breakfast in the morning before they hit the road again.

In summer, if the weather was good and no crop needed attention, Sunday afternoon was a time for farm folks to go visiting. I can still see Mom's reaction when she looked out the window and exclaimed, "Oh, my God! Here come the Mantheys (or the McCanns or the Hanlons), and I don't have anything to give them!" Of course, there were always homemade cookies and snacks on hand, but if they weren't fresh from the oven, they weren't suitable for serving to company. When Sunday visitors arrived, Mom put the coffee pot on the stove, dashed to the living room to check for dust and to the bedroom vanity to tidy up her hair. During the week, visitors were welcomed in the informality of the kitchen. Sunday visitors were formal company and invited into the living room to sit on the upholstered chairs. Sunday visiting was a civilized custom that has faded away, even in Wisconsin. Now people call ahead to be sure to find someone at home and to set a time. The old custom of just dropping in was a more exciting way to keep in touch and catch up on gossip and news.

Though Mom and Dad were always on the lookout for sales and bargains, they were loyal to the stores where they were greeted and waited on by the owner. At Carr's Grocery on Main Street, Mr. Carr waited on us and steered us to the best produce. Willard Woodman greeted us as friends as well as shoppers, even after his little convenience store on Milton Avenue developed into a chain of super-size grocery stores. Familiarity had other rewards. During World War II, Max Meisel took Dad and me to the back of his clothing store to show us a samurai sword and other war booty his soldier son had sent back from the Pacific. For me this was a special treat because I had been closely following the progress of the war.

This small town familiarity and friendliness pervaded our life. Like most farm families, Mom and Dad did not hesitate to help strangers. For example, when a couple whose car had run off the road — in a snowstorm in the middle of the night — came to our door, they were invited in, provided a bed, and in the morning fed a hearty breakfast before Dad got out the tractor and pulled their car out of the ditch. Another time, after watching a luckless hitchhiker stand by our mailbox for over an hour on Thanksgiving Day, Dad invited her in for dinner, and afterwards took her to an intersection where there was more traffic.

During the Depression we shared our house and food with a variety of hired men who worked for room and board and a few a dollars a week. When I was about five, a family of Mexicans, hired to help with our sugar beet crop, lived in a tarpaper shack in the field behind the corncrib. They were there for about a year, but kept to themselves. They never came near our house, but I got my first exposure to international cuisine when, out of curiosity, I walked down to visit and was given pancakes and tortillas. I knew something of pancakes but the tortillas were a new treat for me.

Though I was too small to remember him, Dad often told the story of the "White Russian," a hired man so big and imposing that Mom was afraid of him. Dad fired him on the spot one day when he broke a cardinal rule of our farm. As Dad told the story: "The barn floor was slippery and the horses couldn't get footing to move the loaded manure spreader. This White Russian was yelling and beating the team with a leather whip. I grabbed that whip out of his hand and sent him on his way. He was twice my size and could have taken me apart but he never said a word. He just left." Dad did not put up with mistreatment of animals.

I vaguely remember another hired man who had such a weakness for drink that he broke open my savings bank one night when we were out, took all my savings — about $2.50 — and went to town to quench his thirst. He was a local boy, so we knew his parents. He later came back to repay the money and apologize, but he never worked for us again. Those who got on Dad's bad side usually stayed there.

Dad's major charity effort was Old Henry, a skilled carpenter and a hard worker, but a drinker. Dad never paid him until a job was finished because Henry usually did not show up for work the day after payday. Henry often told Dad he wanted to give up drinking and settle down. Sympathetic, trusting and willing to take a chance, Dad offered him a small plot of land in our woods where he could build a small house, on the condition that he remain sober. Henry accepted and, by himself, built a two-room bungalow and a garage, hooked up electricity and installed a coal stove to heat his 500-square-foot residence. Henry's lot was next to my sister Shirlee, who had married and built a house on Rotamer Road. He carried drinking water from Shirl's well and collected rain water in a barrel for washing. For several years Henry lived a sober life, until one day Shirl came home and found tire tracks running from Henry's driveway, across her lawn, through the ditch and back onto Rotamer Road. Henry had fallen off the water wagon. He was remorseful and, when he sobered up, said he was through drinking. Though he had not kept his part of the bargain, I doubt that Dad ever considered evicting him. Henry was a friend who was doing his best, and that was enough for Dad. Though he had several more relapses over the years, Henry lived in his house until he died in 1971.

For a few years we raised a flock of about 100 ducks. When the ducks were ready for market, Mom and Dad picked and cleaned them and sold them to local stores.

Picking off oily duck feathers is a tedious and time-con-suming job; they don't soften up in boiling water as chicken feathers do. And, once the feathers have been removed, the duck's body is still covered with pin feathers that must be plucked out one by one. To avoid this onerous job, Mom and Dad decided to hold a raffle in the fall of 1940. They mounted a numbered wheel on the wall, invited neighbors, friends and family over, and sold paddles ($1 a paddle) before each spin of the wheel. If the pointer on the wheel stopped at the number on your paddle, you got to take home a live duck from our flock. I think most of the winners knew how much work would be required to prepare that duck for the roasting pan, but some of the city people might have been surprised by the pinfeathers. As the evening went on the chilled beer in a washtub and sandwiches piled on the kitchen table slowly disappeared and cheering for each spin of the wheel grew louder.

Mom had an oyster soup simmering on the cook stove, though not many in that Wisconsin crowd had ever seen an oyster, let alone tried to eat one. I heard a lot of discussion about oysters — where they came from, how they grew, and how to eat them. Inspecting the gray globs in their bowl, some of the women were not sure they could or should be eaten at all. But, before the evening was over, everyone had tried at least one.

The party lasted into the night, far past my bedtime. When I got up the next morning, almost all our ducks were gone. The raffle had been a success, but we never held another. Was it too much work and trouble for the money brought in? Were the ducks just an excuse to have a party? I don't know, nor did I ever ask Mom why she chose to serve oysters that night. Were oysters a passing fad in Wisconsin, or was there just a bargain at the fish market? Whatever the reason, at least it was a way to get people together for a good time and to let someone else deal with the ducks and their pinfeathers.

Most of our entertaining was done with family and close friends on special occasions and holidays — Christmas, Thanksgiving, Easter, and birthdays. These occasions were celebrated with large dinners, always held at noon because most of the guests were farmers who had to be home for evening milking. They were usually hosted by Mom or one of her sisters, either Dell or Mary, who also lived on farms, had big houses, and were used to cooking for large groups. When the dinner was at our house, Mom was up by 6:00 a.m., getting the turkey ready for the oven and organizing the rest of the meal. Dad set up the tables, laid out the silverware, served drinks when guests arrived, and carved the meat when we were ready to eat.

Cars filled our yard by noon. The men moved into the living room to sip beer and talk farming and the women settled in the kitchen to help put the final touches on the meal. The meals were set pieces and followed the same ritual — no matter where the gathering was held. A roast turkey, a ham, and a pork roast graced the table at Christmas and Thanksgiving. At other celebrations, fried chicken replaced the turkey. Along with the meat, there was always mashed potatoes and gravy, cabbage salad, creamed corn, stewed beets, cranberries, olives, celery, and several kinds of pickles. Only the salads that Wisconsin cooks love to create — using Jell-O, whipped cream and fruit — varied, as new recipes were devised and discovered.

Homemade buns were the staple at Mom's meals. The night before the dinner she mixed a huge batch of dough, shaped it into buns, arranged them on trays, covered them with muslin and put them near the stove to rise overnight. She set her alarm, and at 3:00 a.m. she went down to the kitchen to punch the buns down so they would rise one more time and be just right when she got up in the morning to put them in the oven.

When everyone had arrived, the food was arranged on the kitchen table and the children lined up to serve themselves buffet-style, followed by the adults. Then, with loaded plates, everyone found a place at the tables in the dining room and began packing the food in. Mom was always the last person to sit down, but she never stayed seated for long. After a few bites, she was up to help the kids, refill water glasses, replenish a dish, or check on the buffet table. All the while, she encouraged others, "There's plenty of food. Go for a second helping. But be sure to save room for dessert."

We all saved room for dessert, knowing that the choices were staggering. Every dinner had at least Angel food and Devil's food cake, and apple and cherry pie. There was pumpkin pie at Thanksgiving and mincemeat and pecan pie at Christmas. And there was often the Fanning specialty, Schaum Torte, a layer of whipped cream between two layers of crusty meringue, all topped with strawberries. Later in the afternoon Mom would pass around some of her homemade fudge and a box of Fannie Mae candy for those who craved a little more sugar.

When the tables were cleared and the dishes washed, a game or two of euchre would start in the living room. (Euchre is a fast action card game using only a partial deck — nines through aces — and is popular in Wisconsin but rarely played anywhere else.) Those who weren't playing either watched the game or sat in the living room to visit. The festivities always ended about 4:30 p.m., when one of the men would say, "Well, it's getting close to milking time. I guess we better head for home."

"I'll make some sandwiches. No need to do any cooking tonight," Mom would say as she began slipping slices of ham and chicken into leftover buns, wrapping the sandwiches in waxed paper and putting them in a bag with a piece of cake or pie. Soon our kitchen was empty, our yard cleared of cars, and we changed into overalls to do our own evening chores.

Other than family dinners, funerals and weddings, Mom and Dad broke away from their usual pattern of work and sleep by "going out" on a Saturday evening three or four times a year. As they made their plans during the week, there was a building air of excitement. For Shirl and me, it meant a baby-sitter who would play games and let us stay up late. With Dad in a party mood, I could usually wheedle a nickel or dime to send for a Captain Midnight decoder ring or a Tom Mix badge I had heard advertised on the radio.

On their infrequent Saturday evenings out, Mom and Dad dressed in their best clothes and drove to one of the bars on Milton Avenue, usually with another couple, to have a few drinks and dance a fox-trot or a waltz to juke box music on the dance floor in the back room. The luxury of the evening was sitting at a table and being waited on. This was not a wild and crazy outing, even when they were young. They were usually home by midnight, ready to start the work cycle again at 6:00 a.m. Sunday morning.

Dad was not a big drinker, but he was a regular drinker. He enjoyed beer and held it well, but a shot of whiskey made him giddy, and more than one made him sick. Mom was not a drinker at all. In her younger days she sipped a single glass of blackberry brandy all evening, but she never cared for alcohol in any form and soon gave up any pretext of drinking. When they visited a bar, Dad ordered two beers. The bartender put one in front of Mom, where it sat untouched until Dad's glass got low. They then exchanged the glasses and Dad would finish both before ordering two more.

Other than family, Dad's closest friends were our neighbors, Mark Campbell and Art Lucht. The three shared work, tools, and machinery, and when they pooled their skills, they could build anything, fix any piece of machinery, or solve any problem that popped up on a farm.

Art came from Minnesota and had worked in a factory making church pews before he bought the farm just up the road from us. He had a slight Scandinavian accent, and a dry sense of humor. He always seemed to be worrying about the job at hand or the one that was coming. Art's hobby was tinkering and he had an ever-growing collection of tools and equipment in his tool shed. He must have had a tool to build or repair anything ever made, but there was no order to his collection and only he knew where to look for it. After he sold his herd of dairy cows and retired from farming, Art devoted himself to full-time tinkering. One day he laid the hot tip of a welder too near a pile of straw and burned down his barn. He took the loss with his usual aplomb. "Well," he reasoned, "The cows are gone. I don't need a barn now anyway."

Mark had broader interests. He read magazines other than *The Farm Journal,* was interested in what was happening in the world and had an opinion on every subject. He had a ruddy complexion and a rolling walk that made me think he was always negotiating the side of a hill. Even in the heat of summer he wore long wool underwear, claiming they soaked up the sweat and kept him cool. I didn't have the temerity to suggest that if he got rid of the wool longies he wouldn't sweat as much.

In the early 1960's, Interstate 90 was built between Mark and Art's farm, taking several acres of their land and netting them enough federal funds to retire. Unfortunately, Mark died of cancer in 1963, an untimely and tragic passing in a family that had suffered too many untimely deaths. (Mark's first wife died in childbirth in the mid-1930's. His youngest brother, John, went to the Philippines with the Wisconsin National Guard unit in 1941, was captured by the Japanese and died of malaria in a prison camp in 1942. Another brother, Hank, operated a successful bar on Milton Avenue, loved flying, and became a skilled pilot. He and his wife were killed in northern Wisconsin in 1953, when they crashed in a heavy thunderstorm.)

Weddings, funerals, births and illnesses were important elements in our lives. When Mom opened the Janesville Gazette each afternoon, the first thing she checked was the social page, which listed births, deaths, marriages and the names of those admitted and discharged from Mercy Hospital. If a close friend was in the hospital, Mom and Dad went to visit right after milking. Visiting the sick was a friendly act and a social obligation. In his later years, Dad went almost every day to visit one of "the old guys," friends who were laid up from accident, poor health or age, even though most were younger than he.

Mom and Dad considered it impolite to miss a funeral and their names must be inscribed in almost every memorial book in Rock County. For close friends they attended both the visitation at the funeral home and the funeral. For those they didn't know well they attended one or the other. Funerals were a time to offer condolences to the family and to show one's respect for the deceased. They were also social events, chances to catch up on news from old schoolmates, relatives, and acquaintances who would not otherwise have gathered in one place.

Chapter 12
Mom and Dad

Mom cooked three meals a day, cleaned the house, made the beds, did the laundry, tended the chickens, and helped Dad whenever she could, but she always found time to make treats and desserts. After school, Shirl and I could always look forward to a pile of cookies fresh from the oven or a batch of doughnuts puffing up in the hot grease on the stove. For special occasions Mom made her special buns (later known as "Grandma buns"), a Schaum Torte, or a batch of fudge — and usually all three. During my years in the navy my shipmates shadowed me at mail call to see if I got a box of fudge or chocolate chip cookies from Mom. When mail was handed out I had no way of hiding the square boxes Mom used to send treats, so I really had no choice but to share them with my hungry shipmates.

Although Mom enjoyed cooking, baking and working at outside jobs, her passion was communicating — in person, in notes and letters, and by phone. I think her lengthy conversations on our party line were her recreation, a chance to socialize in a time when it was not easy to get together in person. She talked with the neighbors, with her sisters, with childhood friends, and with ladies she had worked with in town before she was married. Until rotary phones, Mom was tethered to the big phone that hung on the dining room wall, holding the receiver to her ear and speaking into the mouthpiece that protruded from the wooden frame. When we got a dial phone in the 1950s, Mom put it in the kitchen and attached a flexible cord long enough to let her move to the sink, the stove or the table — so she could work while she talked, or vice versa.

Mom preparing buns for the oven

Mom used the telephone as a link to the world beyond the farm and her phone conversations were lengthy. We were on a party line, that is, several homes were served by the same phone line. If you picked up the phone and heard someone talking, you were expected to wait until they finished. Only in an emergency did one ask for the line. Conversations on a party line were often long because there was a lot of information to be passed around. If an interesting story was being told when Mom checked the line, it was hard to hang up before hearing the end. Listening in was another way of hearing the news while passing the time, something like watching the local news on the radio. Whether listening in was inadvertent or not, silence was important so that the listener would not be detected. Hearing the storyteller say, "I think someone is listening in. I'll call you later," then promptly hanging-up, was very disappointing, especially if the story was near conclusion.

Mom on the phone in the kitchen

Mom was an avid letter writer, sending personal notes for any event — birth, death, anniversary, graduation, or illness. She wrote to neighbors and friends who had moved away. She even began a correspondence with the son of a friend who was in prison, because she was afraid no one else would write to him. Her regular letters kept me up to date on family news and local developments while I was in the Navy and later when I was overseas with the State Department. Though we talked often on the phone when I was living in Virginia, she still wrote at least one newsy letter every week. Not until her 95th year did her perfect penmanship become a little shaky and her sentences begin to ramble. During her last months, when she was hardly able to finish a thought or a sentence, she still tried to add a personal note on the birthday cards Shirl helped her send to grandchildren and great-grandchildren.

Dad was only comfortable communicating in person. His writing was limited to methodically writing out checks, lists and reminders to himself in a crabbed hand. As far as I know, he wrote just one letter in his life - to me, in 1951, when I was in boot camp at Great Lakes Naval Training Station north of Chicago. In pencil, on a single sheet of lined paper, he told me March weather had been good and the corn crop was in. He hoped everything was going all right for me in the navy. I can imagine how Mom must have pushed him to write that letter and the effort it took for him to do it. I am sorry I did not keep that letter, but at the time I didn't realize it was something special.

Dad was equally uncomfortable using the telephone. His phone conversations were only for business and never lasted more than a minute. When I called long distance, we only exchanged a couple of words about the weather before he asked, "Do you want to talk to Mom?" and turned the phone over to her.

Sports like baseball, hunting, and fishing bored him,

but Dad gladly joined with friends who did those things because he liked the company. Occasionally, in the spring, he hired someone to do the milking and went up north with two or three friends for the smelt run. Smelt are small fish, about two inches long, that are netted out of streams as they move to spawning grounds. Dad's group left after lunch and returned late the next morning looking tired and hung over, with buckets of the tiny fish in the trunk of the car. Smelt are tasty but spoil quickly, so Mom quickly cleaned and fried up our share of the catch. We ate what we could and threw out the rest. When it came to smelt, the trip was the important thing.

Dad kept two shotguns — a small caliber, single-shot .410-gauge and a 12-gauge repeater — mainly to kill weasels, foxes and skunks that tried to get our chickens. He rarely went into our fields to hunt, but was always ready to ride around the countryside with friends in the fall, with a shotgun on the back seat, looking for pheasants or ducks. When I was about 12, I was invited along for the ride — or so I thought. He stopped the car when we came upon a flock of ducks feeding in a cornfield, braced the shotgun against the door, and told me to get one of those ducks for dinner. This was my first time with such a big gun, and I was nervous and uncertain as I picked out a target, lined up the sight, and pulled the trigger. The blast startled both me and the ducks. My shot landed well short of the flock, which took off with a flurry and was well out of range before I could pump out the spent shell and load another.

Dad took me hunting once — a short excursion through the fields behind the barn. He probably thought it was time I learned the fundamentals of the sport. We walked through the cornfield, north toward the woods, looking for rabbits or pheasants. Dad carried the 12-gauge and I had the .410. The 12-gauge held six shells which could be fired consecutively, the old shell was expelled, a fresh one loaded, and the hammer cocked by pumping a lever on the bottom of the barrel. The .410 held a single shell and the hammer had to be pulled back and locked in place before the gun could be fired. When the hammer was cocked, accidental pressure on the trigger or a sudden jolt would set off. "Don't walk with the hammer cocked," Dad cautioned, "Cock it only when you're ready to fire. You don't want it to go off by accident." When a rabbit jumped out of a corn stubble by my feet, I began to raise the gun to my shoulder while pushing on the hammer with my thumb. But cold hands, wet gloves, and a little anxiety caused my thumb to slip off the hammer before it locked. It snapped back, hit the firing pin, and the gun went off with a roar, blowing a hole in the ground not far in front me. I was startled and shaken, and thought, "Damn, this is dangerous. I might have hit Dad or blown my own foot off." Dad hadn't seen that my shot had been a dangerous mistake and I didn't tell him. To my relief we didn't see any more game that day and Dad never suggested we go hunting again. He might have thought I had learned enough about the sport, or maybe he saw that shooting guns did not excite me and realized I was not destined to be a hunter.

Practical jokes were one of Dad's biggest diversions. At wedding receptions he would sneak out to the newlyweds' car and wire a device to a spark plug that whistled, exploded with a bang, and filled the car with smoke when the car was started. Or he and his friends would sneak into the house of recently married couples (not difficult, because no one locked their doors) and put corn flakes under the sheets so they would have an uncomfortable night when they got home from their honeymoon.

When out drinking with friends, Dad often suggested to his drinking companions that one of them should throw a glass to get a bartender's attention. One evening in a Milton Avenue bar he took off his shoe and threw it at a friend. The shoe missed its target and landed on the back bar, breaking several bottles of expensive whiskey. Dad went back the next morning to make amends and pay for the breakage. "I don't know what came over me," he told the owner, though it is likely both the action — and his poor aim — came late in an evening of beer and banter.

Dad was usually first on the scene when disaster struck and he developed a reputation for helping anyone in need. He was the first one to show up the morning after a neighbor's house burned to help the family salvage what they could. When he left, he told them, "If there is anything I can do to help, just call." Fifty years later, those neighbors still recall Dad's compassion and willingness to help.

At home, Dad was less communicative than when he was with his friends. At meals we talked about school, teachers, homework and activities, but I think most of the time his mind was on work to be done, machinery that needed repair, and making the money stretch till the next milk check. When something was bothering him, he closed into silence. "I wonder what's bothering him now?" Mom would mutter. He was one to not talk about his problems so we just waited, knowing he would work it out himself after a time.

Dad teaches grandson Peter to ride

Mom took care of the routine activities for Shirl and me — getting us to school, making sure we did our homework, taking us to the doctor and the dentist, and shopping for clothes. Dad handled only the emergencies: a trip to the doctor with Shirl when she was hit in the head by a swing , and doctor visits with me when I stepped on a nail, gashed my foot on a rock, and slashed the end of my thumb with a new jack knife. He was not one for comforting words on the way to the doctor, but he held me gently as the doctor stitched my thumb without anesthesia.

Mom was the first line of discipline - rule maker and rule enforcer. She didn't hesitate to whack my butt when I disobeyed or gave her trouble. I could get away with quite a bit, but when she called me a "little shitass," I knew I had gone too far and prepared myself for a spanking. She used this term of deep disapproval on me until I was at least fourteen and I was not surprised when she applied the same term to her grandsons. It was still part of her vocabulary when her great grandson did something to displease her.

She had other vivid phrases, as well. "I sat there like a frozen turd" cannot be improved on to describe inaction brought on by fear or frigid temperature, and "scared fartless" aptly describes ones reaction to a fright. When unable to make progress on a job she said she was "just fart-diddling around." And farmers knew exactly what color Dad had in mind when he described a new car as "calf-shit yellow." At first I was embarrassed when Mom or Dad dropped one of these descriptive gems in conversation with my friends. Now I realize how fine and accurate they are and I miss hearing them.

A farm is a dangerous place and Shirl and I were given clear and emphatic instructions on what to do to avoid accidents: Don't enter a cow pasture if you don't know where the bull is; be alert and cautious when working near machinery; never do anything that might surprise an animal, especially when approaching from the rear; and always shut down machinery before trying to repair any part of it. Although we paid close attention to these rules, Dad often ignored them when he was in a hurry. Over the years, accidents with machinery and animals left him with a swollen elbow, a twisted wrist, scarred hands, and crooked fingers. When he lost the tips of two fingers on his right hand to the sickle of the combine, he drove the truck to the house to get help. I had to clean the blood from the shifting lever and the floor before we could use the truck again. "It was my own damned fault," he said as he stood in the entry way, his hand wrapped in a bloody towel, changing his clothes before going to the hospital. (We never left the farm in work clothes except for a quick trip to the feed mill or blacksmith shop.) "I had a sandwich in my hand and reached down to flip a piece of dirt out of the sickle. I should have turned it off. Here, help me get this belt fastened so we can get started. This damned towel gets in the way." As a friend drove us to the hospital he groused, "Slow down a little. I don't want to get killed on the highway over something like this." In the emergency room the doctor cleaned and sewed the wounds and told Dad he would have to stay in the hospital overnight. All evening Dad fretted about the crop of oats that stood ripe in the field. He needn't have worried. When we brought him home the next day four neighbors were in our field with their combines and our oats were in the granary before the sun went down.

Dad was tough and resilient, working outside in sub-zero temperatures and 95-degree heat, remarking only about how the temperature affected animals and equipment. For 35 years, he milked the cows and did the chores no matter how he felt. Some days he moved a little slower, or looked a little pale, but he never took a day off or complained that he was sick. If he was under the weather he probably took a nap in the hay, though no one ever saw him do it. "He didn't have any feelings, inside or out," Mom said once. This was not really true, but it often appeared that way. Dad ignored discomfort and pain and was a stranger to tender words and gestures, though he was a good friend and good Samaritan to those who were sick or in need.

Chapter 13

Farewell to the Farm

It was music that set my life on a course away from the farm. Mom always had the radio tuned to popular music when she was working in the kitchen and she must have been the one who insisted Shirl and I take music lessons, because I never heard Dad whistle, sing or hum a tune. Shirl began on piano and I took up the accordion. I don't remember if I chose the accordion or if it was chosen for me in the hope that I would carry it to dinners and picnics to entertain family and friends. If the latter was true, I fell far short of that goal. An accordion is a heavy and ungainly instrument, requiring concentration and coordination to play. Though otherwise fairly well-coordinated, I could not get the knack of squeezing the bellows, fingering the keyboard with my right hand and pushing the chord buttons with my left. I tried for several weeks, with diminishing enthusiasm, until one day Dad said, "Either practice those lessons or quit." We returned the accordion to the store.

But I didn't lose interest in music. It was the era of big bands and I loved the power and clarity of trumpeters like Harry James and Louis Armstrong. Trumpets soared above the rest of the orchestra and I thought, "This is the horn for me." I begged Mom to forget the accordion fiasco and to let me try trumpet lessons. She agreed, and from my first off-pitch blast on the horn I was hooked. I loved to prac-

tice and I loved to play. In high school I slighted academics
and concentrated on the band. My friends were band members, my best grades were in band, and I began to think that
I might have a future in music.

Until I became infatuated with music, I had always
assumed that my future naturally lay somewhere in Rock
County, where I would continue farming (in one way or
another). Except for the rigid milking routines of a dairy
farm, I enjoyed the challenges and independence of farming.
To prepare myself, I took agriculture courses in high school
and joined the Future Farmers of America — an organization
that prepared students for a career in agriculture. But farming seemed to be in my future primarily because I could see
no alternative. The history and adventure books I read and
the exciting radio programs I listened to had left me with a
curiosity about how people in other parts of the country
lived and worked, and I secretly hoped that something would
come along that would give me a chance to try something
different. As my love of music and the trumpet continued to
grow, I began to think that they might become my "magic
carpet" away from the farm.

They did, but not quite in the way I imagined. The
Korean War began in June 1950, the month and year of my
high school graduation. Searching for an alternative to being
drafted into the army, I heard that the navy had a music
school that trained musicians for assignment to bands all
over the world. Mom encouraged me to look into it but
said, "You'd better check with Dad before you apply." So
Dad and I had one of our direct and succinct conversations.
"Dad," I said, "I'd like to join the navy and get into the
music program." "If that's what you want to do, OK," he
replied, and the conversation was over. We had just agreed

to a turning point in both our lives. I was probably leaving the farm for good, and Dad would have to take on all the work I had shouldered over the years. But the decision was made, and I looked forward to starting a new adventure.

However, in February 1951, two weeks before I was to report to Great Lakes Naval Station near Chicago for boot camp, fire visited our farm once again. Mom shook me awake in the middle of the night, shouting, "Get up, Bob, the chicken house is on fire!" Orange reflections danced on my bedroom wall as I hurriedly dressed. When I got outside both the chicken house and the pig shed next to it were burning. Dad was calmly wetting down the granary (only 30 feet away from the flames) with the fire extinguisher, though he must have been thinking of the conflagration that had taken its toll 19 years before. Mom had called the Janesville fire department, but our road was blocked by drifting snow, the aftermath of a blizzard that had just passed through. We could see the flashing red lights of the fire truck a mile away as it sat idling, waiting for a snowplow. There wasn't much we could do but hope that the fire did not spread. When the fire truck finally arrived, the fires had all but burned themselves out. The firemen checked the other buildings for smoldering embers and wet down the pile of rubble that used to be the chicken house and pig shed. Seventy pigs and more than 150 chickens had been in the buildings. They, too, were lost.

I had been six-months old when our buildings went up in flames in 1932. Nineteen years later, as if to bookend my time on the farm, another fire had struck. But the buildings and the livestock were insured; Dad would rebuild. He never once suggested that I change my plans because of the fire. Two weeks later Mom and Dad drove me to Great Lakes to start my new life.

So music was finally taking me away from the farm, though the magic carpet turned out to be an aircraft carrier, the USS Boxer. I went through eight weeks of boot camp, then spent a year at the Navy School of Music in Washington, D.C. On graduation I was assigned to the band on the Boxer and sailed for Korea in March, 1952. The Boxer operated with the 7th Fleet off Korea for six weeks to two months at a time, then spent two to three weeks in port in Yokosuka, Japan. Our versatile 16-piece band played daily concerts on the hangar deck, all-day sessions of marches while we refueled at sea, and dance jobs at navy clubs when we were in port. After an armistice ended the ground war in Korea, we sailed south to visit Hong Kong and Manila. During my three years on the Boxer I discovered two things that set the course of my life: that I was a good trumpet player, but did not have the musical talent needed for a successful career in music, and that Asia was a dynamic and fascinating place — a place I wanted to know more about.

In 1955, I returned home, navy discharge in hand, and enrolled in the University of Wisconsin. The GI Bill covered my tuition, books and basic expenses, and two or three dance band jobs a week provided money for beer, dates and dinners out. I played with a dance orchestra at local country clubs, with Dixieland jazz groups at fraternity parties on campus, and in halls all over southern Wisconsin with the Shamrock Polka Band. During my five years at UW I lived in Madison, but gladly went home to help with milking and field work on weekends. This was, to some extent, payment to Mom and Dad for letting me choose my own life and set my own goals. It was also a chance to load my car with food on Sunday evenings, enough to carry me through a week of study. In 1959, I received a BA degree in history and in the fall of 1960, an MA in Asian studies. I said goodbye to the farm for the last time and headed for Washington, D.C., and a foreign service career in Asia with the U.S. Information Agency.

Chapter 14

The Last Harvest

In 1968, after farming for more than 50 years, Dad decided to retire. He sold the dairy herd, rented the farm land to a friend, and sold the 40-acres of woods to a developer. But, like his father, he discovered that farmers can't just up and walk away from the work and the land. He remained active, helping friends with field work and fixing things around the farm. Over the years, a developing heart condition sapped his strength and he gradually cut back on heavy work.

When Dad reached 80, he found it harder to keep up with routine maintenance. Nature encroached on places he had always kept neat and clean when it was a working farm. Weeds grew up thick and tall around rusting machinery behind the barn. Wind, rain and snow ate away at the buildings; paint began to chip, peel and flake. Wooden shingles on the vast expanse of barn roof split and blew off, letting in rain to collect on the floor of the haymow. Mom and Dad repaired and painted the board fences around the yard, but over the years the posts rotted off and the fences sagged out of line. Though deterioration was gradual and barely perceptible at first, the farm had lost its purpose and was aging along with Dad. To restore it to life required money, but how could a retired farmer justify spending on buildings that would never be used again?

It bothered Dad when he saw houses being built in the woods he had sold to finance retirement. The good black dirt that had provided bountiful crops for more than 100 years would now nurture nothing more significant than lawns and landscaping. Mom said that each morning he looked out the kitchen window toward the woods and asked aloud, "Why did I sell that land to that developer?"

On December 27, 1990, just after his 86th birthday, Dad drove to his cardiologist for a regular checkup. The doctor looked at the electrocardiogram and said, "You're on the verge of a major heart attack. You are going to the hospital immediately." He was sent by ambulance to Meritor Hospital in Madison. Although his cardiologist had warned him for years of a deteriorating heart valve, Dad had refused surgery. But when the Meritor doctor told him he would be bedridden if he didn't replace a calcified valve, Dad agreed to the operation. He could not abide the thought of inactivity for the rest of his life. The operation was successful but, two weeks later, when he was almost recovered, he suffered a major stroke. He died on January 21, 1991.

Even though the old house was drafty and cold in winter, Mom was determined to stay on the farm after Dad died, and she would have, if the State of Wisconsin had not decided to widen Highway 14. A letter from the Department of Transportation announced that the state would pay a fair price for the house, but that Mom would have to move and the house would be demolished. Mom used the state payment to build a new house next to Shirl on Rotamer Road. It was not easy to leave the house she had lived in for 65 years, but she did not complain or break down. As we emptied drawers and packed boxes before the move, I asked Mom, "How can you take this so calmly?" She replied, "I just made up my mind that it had to be done and I don't think about it." That was the way we did things in our family.

Mom began to slow down when she reached 95 — but only a little bit. She still liked to keep herself busy. Once, when she was in the hospital for dehydration and heart problems, a nurse asked Shirl what Mom did for recreation. Mom didn't knit, watch television, or read novels. So, when nothing else came to mind, Shirl said, "She works." And soon, during her "recovery," Mom was contentedly folding hospital sheets that the staff brought to her room.

As I gathered ideas for this memoir I once asked Mom what she most remembered about life on the farm during the Depression. "It was hard work," she said. Then, after some reflection, she added, "But it was fun." Dad probably would have said the same.

Mom passed away peacefully in her own bed on February 5, 2003.

Chapter 15

Memories

After Mom died I took a long walk around our old property. All that was left of the once-vibrant farm was 55 acres of land and several farm buildings badly in need of repair. There was no spirit, no life left in it.

A bare spot at the edge of the yard was the only visible reminder of the house that had stood there for more than 100 years. The barn was only a shell. The rows of stanchions were still there — gutter behind and manger in front — but covered with rust. The empty silo echoed the chirps and flutters of sparrows, while pigeons and swallows had made their nests in the rafters of the cavernous haymow.

I missed the rich farm odors I had ignored in my youth: the sweet smell of fresh hay, the sour scent of silage, even the distinctive odors of horse, cow, calf, pig, and chicken manure. And the remaining buildings still conjured memories of animals raised, crops grown and stored, and of the incredible amount of work Mom and Dad put into running the farm over the years.

But they were memories lacking a core. Without the central presence of the house, I was unable to connect the dilapidating farm to my youth. It was no longer my home; it was really no longer a farm. It was just a small island of arable land that most people saw as potential lots for houses. There were houses to the north, east and south, and to the west was a shopping mall. Our land had already been annexed into the city of Janesville. There was no way we could preserve this small area of farm land any more.

When Shirl and I decided to finally sell the remaining land in 2004, we also decided that the the farm and our parents should be remembered in some way. The Janesville Parks Department had already set aside as a nature reserve the area around the pond where our cattle gathered every afternoon to drink before coming home to milking. This seemed to us to be an ideal spot for a memorial. The head of the Parks Department enthusiastically supported our plan. Shirl and I designed and had cast a bronze plaque and, with the assistance of the Parks Department, had it mounted on a boulder taken from a nearby field.

On April 16, 2005, one hundred people — family, friends, former neighbors, and nearby residents — joined Shirl and me in dedicating the boulder and the plaque. It was a clear spring day, like many of the days we had spent on the farm in our youth. We will look back fondly on those days each time we read the inscription on the plaque:

In Memory of Alfred and Helen Knopes

Who, from their marriage in 1930 until 1991,
operated a 160-acre dairy farm that stretched from
Highway 14 to Rotamer Road. In summer months,
their dairy herd grazed in the woodlands beyond
and every afternoon gathered at this pond to drink.
Homes and streets have replaced the farm, but this
park remnant preserves a special place, when, in
days gone by, the sounds of frogs, cows, and birds
filled the air.

Shirl and me at the dedication
of the memorial to our parents

ANY DAMN FOOL CAN BE A FARMER

BOB KNOPES

ANY DAMN FOOL CAN BE A FARMER

Printed in the United States
202398BV00003B/1-153/A